Saint John Neumann

WONDER-WORKER OF PHILADELPHIA

Recent Miracles
1961 - 1991

by Father Timothy E. Byerley

Grant of Approval by the
Most Reverend James T. McHugh, S.T.D.
Bishop of Camden
Given at Camden, New Jersey
April 29, 1992

Cover by Rena Sinakin

Library of Congress catalogue
number 92-62045
ISBN 0-9634825-0-5

To The Blessed Virgin Mary,

St. John Neumann's

Beloved Heavenly Mother

and Protectress

TABLE OF CONTENTS

PREFACE

Hundreds and hundreds of people claim to have received favors from heaven through the intercession of St. John Neumann, the fourth bishop of Philadelphia who died in 1860. This book highlights some of the most recent and dramatic of the miracles attributed to the holy bishop. The persons who received these favors were willing to permit them to be reported so that others who find themselves in situations of disappointment, suffering, sorrow and sickness will have reason to hope. As these stories demonstrate, "the favors of the Lord are not exhausted, his mercies are not spent, they are renewed each morning, so great is his faithfulness." (Lam 3:22-23) Nearly all of the accounts in this book were given to the author first hand (the exceptions are noted in the text). All are supported by written testimonies. Everything is a matter of public record so that those who wish to examine and verify the stories can do so. Most, but not all, of these miraculous graces were granted to individuals who have some connection with the city of Philadelphia. Just as the people of Naples consider St. Januarius the protector-saint of their city, one wonders if St. John Neumann, the first man from the United States to be canonized, isn't the heavenly protector and caretaker of Philadelphia. Be that as it may, special thanks must go to Fr. Fehrenbach, coordinator at the St. John Neumann Shrine*, for making available the files of reported miracles** and for his constant and generous efforts in supporting this endeavor. His secretary, Rita McGuigan, has been equally supportive in rendering such kind assistance. Suzanne Brownholtz is also to be thanked for her painstaking review of the text. Finally, a word of gratitude goes to Bernadette Smutko for her typing of the manuscript. Most of all, a heart-felt appreciation is expressed to all those who consented to have their stories included in this book. May many, many persons gain strength and encouragement from their testimonies.

* The St. John Neumann Shrine is located in St. Peter's Redemptorist Church at Fifth Street and Girard Avenue in Philadelphia.
** See Appendix I for theological definition of a miracle.

INTRODUCTION

In the beginning of the New Year of 1860, Bishop Neumann uncharacteristically admitted to not feeling well. On Thursday, January 5, 1860, Bishop Neumann was taking lunch with his auxiliary bishop James Wood in the dining room of his Cathedral rectory on Race Street at Logan Circle in central Philadelphia. Bishop Wood recalled that Neumann related an anecdote about the simplicity of life in his Bohemian homeland at table that day. After lunch Bishop Neumann received a surprise visit from an old friend, Fr. Urbanczik, C.SS.R. When the priest was ushered into the Bishop's presence, he was taken aback by the lackluster appearance in Neumann's eyes. Fr. Urbanczik inquired if he was sick. Bishop Neumann answered, "I have a strange feeling today. I never felt this way before. I have to go out on a little business, and the fresh air will do me good." The Bishop set out for a lawyer's office to sign a deed connected with some church property. It was a chilly day. Returning home he walked across the street at Vine near Thirteenth in Old Philadelphia. His gait became unsteady. He staggered and fell on the steps of one of the private residences. Two men rushed to help him and carried him into the house of a non-Catholic, but it was too late. Bishop Neumann expired at 3:00 PM. He was forty-eight years old. All of Philadelphia mourned. His funeral was held on January 9, 1860. People said it was the greatest funeral throng in the history of the city. Even during Neumann's lifetime, religious pictures and goods received from his hands were carefully preserved, and scraps of his clothes were held as precious relics. After his death, however, the desire to possess articles belonging to him became feverish. The opinion among the faithful was that Bishop Neumann's life had been that of a saint. Soon after his death, a number of Catholics began kneeling reverently near his grave, presenting their spiritual and temporal needs to him. According to his nephew, Fr. John A. Berger, C.SS.R., who wrote Neumann's first biography in 1882, graces were already being granted. Fr. Berger writes: "Of the prayers thus answered we have innumerable accounts attested by trustworthy witnesses. We have been informed, also, of many wonderful cures affected through the holy bishop's intercession." These reports, which flourished immediately after his death, have continued unmitigated to this present day. Contained in the following pages the reader will find a noteworthy sample of great favors ascribed to St. John Neumann.*

---

* Intercession is the theological principle whereby a person in need appeals to a holy soul, living or deceased, to present his petition to God. The understanding is that the holy soul is more likely to receive for the petitioner this grace, given his unique intimacy with the Lord. This principle is amply supported by the Scriptures and Christian Tradition.

I

PRO-LIFE BISHOP

St. John Neumann, when he was bishop of Philadelphia in the 1850's courageously addressed a number of moral issues. But life issues did not require any serious attention at the time. In those days everyone — Protestant, Catholic, Jew, Gentile — all considered human life sacred. It was a non-issue.

Would St. John Neumann have anything to say about life issues if he were a bishop in the United States today? Apparently he would. The following three stories demonstrate where St. John Neumann stands on issues regarding the sanctity of human life.

The first two stories deal with unborn babies. The third shows the impropriety of terminating life before natural death.

Bishop Neumann, even from heaven, is teaching us that human life is inviolable from the moment of conception to the moment of natural death. For this reason he can be called a pro-life bishop.

BABY NICHOLAS

It is the custom in Philadelphia, which has such a large Catholic population, to identify neighborhoods by the parish within whose boundaries the neighborhood lies. So when Donna and Stephen Spadaccini say that they are from St. Richard's parish in South Philly, Philadelphians know that they live down in the shadow of Veteran's Stadium, home of the Philadelphia Eagles and Phillies sports teams. On a clear night the Spadaccinis can see the white aurora of the stadium lights illuminating the skies of south Philadelphia and hear the distant roar of the Philadelphia sports fans cheering and booing (they are known as the "boo-birds" because of how vociferous they can be in their disapproval of players and officials).

In early winter 1991, however, Donna and Stephen were not thinking much about the Philadelphia Eagles. Married four years, in their late 20's, they were expecting their second child. In Donna's sixteenth week of pregnancy a routine blood test revealed a high level of protein in her blood. This suggested that a defect in the baby in her womb was causing protein to leak from his body into her bloodstream.

Her obstetrician at Pennsylvania Hospital conducted further tests. The results indicated a chromosomal abnormality which caused a perforation in the baby's body. In these types of cases it is usually a perforation in the head or the spine. It was likely that the baby would die immediately upon birth.

Donna was given "genetic counseling" and her doctor strongly advised her to "terminate the pregnancy." Donna responded with equivalent strength, "That is not an option for us under any circumstances. I will not abort my child. My husband and I agree, we will deal with whatever happens."

News of the Spadaccini's difficulties spread among their family and friends. Two of her best friends' relatives from South Philadelphia began offering prayers to St. John Neumann and visiting the saint's shrine at St.

Peter's church on Fifth Street and Girard Avenue on behalf of the Spadaccini baby. Donna also started her own novena to St. John Neumann.

A second battery of tests was administered in order to better identify the problem. Ultrasound and amniocentesis procedures showed the perforation to be in the baby's stomach. Loops of bowel protruded through his abdomen wall and skin, actually extending outside his body. The liver began to work its way outside the perforation also.

If he lived he would be small, never normal. He might have to carry a colostomy bag around with him for the rest of his life, however brief it might be. Corrective surgery would be needed immediately upon birth, and a one to five month recovery period would be required if he survived delivery. He might even die in the womb.

Again her doctor strongly recommended "terminating the pregnancy." Donna was adamant; she would hear none of this kind of talk. She was insulted by these recommendations and lost respect for her doctor. This was her obstetrician, the one who was supposed to be helping her bring her pregnancy to term, and here he was strongly advising her to put an end to her child's life. She was "disappointed in him for the rest of the pregnancy."

But Donna had other help. When her friends began their novena to St. John Neumann they also gave her a first class relic of the saint. Donna wore this relic around her waist for three weeks, soon after the first bad report about the baby's condition surfaced. After that she frequently blessed her womb with the relic and continued her requests for St. John Neumann's intercession.

Every three weeks ultrasound tests were done to check the baby's growth and development. He progressed normally despite the defect. The doctors were encouraged.

Then, at seven and one-half months something strange occurred. The defect could not be found in the ultrasound scans. The technician was confused. He went immediately to the perinatalogist (pre-natal doctor). The perinatalogist confirmed that all of the baby's organs and bowels were entirely restored to their proper place inside the abdomen wall, which was now closed. Only a slight protrusion of skin remained. The perinatalogist was confounded. "This isn't supposed to happen," he said.

The doctors at Pennsylvania Hospital discussed in bewilderment how this healing could have taken place spontaneously, without medical intervention, over a three month period. The usual progression in these cases is just the opposite, with the intestines and organs continuing to extrude outside the abdomen.

Nicholas was born two weeks early. The doctors induced labor because they felt it best not to wait any longer. Six doctors were in the delivery room. All were ready, prepared for the worst. At 10:45 AM on May 9, 1991 Nicholas

Spadaccini was born perfectly normal, save a little blister of skin on his stomach. The six doctors on hand were so happy and exuberant that they swept up baby Nicholas and rushed out of the delivery room, huddling around Nicholas like he was a great prize. The doctors shuffled down the hallway as one, gleefully showing him to colleagues and nurses at the various units.

"The mother!" They suddenly realized that they had left an equally happy mother and grandmother in the delivery room all alone. They hurried back and Donna took her healthy, seven-pound, four-ounce baby and tenderly enveloped him in her arms with the supreme satisfaction and joy that only a mother can know.

The emergency stand-by unit which had been on call was dismissed. A few days later Nicholas was transported to Philadelphia's Children's Hospital for the removal of the blister, a minor procedure. Dr. Ross, the surgeon at Children's Hospital, could not understand why there were no side effects from Nicholas's in-utero complications either.

Today Nicholas is doing very well and is perfectly normal. Donna believes that her obstetrician is grateful that she did not take his advice to terminate Nicholas.

Reflecting on the whirlwind of events and all the prayers that were offered for Nicholas, Donna believes that the purpose of it all was to bring people to God. So many family members, friends, in-laws, co-workers and even doctors were touched by Nicholas's recovery. Even Donna's employer, a Jewish doctor, prayed for Nicholas. Many of these people have since returned to Sunday Mass and confession, and a serious life of faith.

And, by the way, Donna and Stephen have given Nicholas a middle name: John. ■

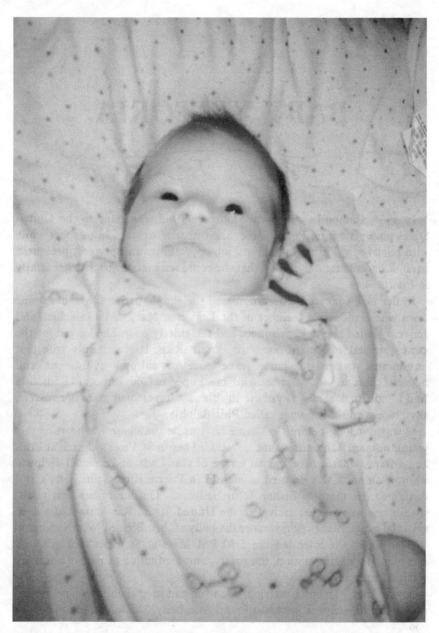

"Miracle baby" Nicholas Spadaccini of South Philadelphia, born May 9, 1991.

BABY VICTORIA

In 1964, Ramonita was twenty-four years old, she came to the United States on a visit from Puerto Rico. She intended to stay only a short while with relatives in Philadelphia, but a job opportunity unexpectedly presented itself. Ramonita took the job so that she could send money back to her family in Puerto Rico.

In her new country Ramonita missed the simple parish life of her home town where she was a member of the Legion of Mary and a catechist, and actively visited the sick, prisoners and the elderly poor. She longed for the same spiritual solace she knew in Puerto Rico. It is certainly true that immigrants suffer the harsh experience of cultural adjustment and homesickness and for this reason are more open to God. But could Ramonita find a "spiritual home" anywhere in this vast impersonal maze of concrete, skyscrapers and row homes called Philadelphia?

It was not long before God came to console the homesick heart of this young woman. Ramonita's aunt introduced her to St. Peter's church at Fifth and Girard, where there was an image of Our Lady of Perpetual Help, to whom Ramonita was devoted as a child in Puerto Rico. Saint Peter's also contained the tomb of Bishop John Neumann. On one of her first visits, within one week of her arrival in the United States, Ramonita had a deep spiritual experience praying before the body of then Blessed John Neumann.

Ever since, she attended the 5:30 PM Mass at St. Peter's church and included Holy Communion, the rosary, and meditation as part of her daily spiritual routine.

A year later Ramonita married; soon she had several children and settled in North Philadelphia near Ninth and Allegheny. She was in the States for good.

Over the years Bishop Neumann helped her in many different ways. But in 1989 she was calling on him for special assistance. Ramonita's unmarried daughter had conceived a child and was not taking proper care of herself. She wouldn't eat properly or take her medication or vitamins during her pregnancy. But Ramonita was even more alarmed by her imprudent physical exertion and rough play. Ramonita became seriously concerned about her future grandchild's well-being, but her headstrong daughter was not to be deterred. Ramonita felt helpless.

Daily she poured out her heart at the shrine. Many nights, when her daughter was asleep, Ramonita would quietly slip into her room with a first class relic of St. John Neumann and touch it to her daughter's forehead and abdomen, in hopes that the good Bishop would counter the negative effects of her daughter's improper pre-natal care. In the darkness of her daughter's bedroom she would whisper to St. John Neumann, "You be her nourishment."

On May 27, Ramonita was attending a parish mission at St. Veronica's, her parish church in North Philadelphia. Her other children (young adults at the time) came quickly up the aisle of St. Veronica's church to their mother's pew to tell her that their sister was rushed to Temple University Hospital, hemorrhaging heavily. She had just given birth to a five month premature girl weighing only one pound, ten ounces. Both mother and child were in serious condition.

Ramonita called on her parish priest at St. Veronica's rectory, who went directly to Temple University Hospital and baptized baby Victoria. By this time Ramonita's daughter was out of danger, but her granddaughter, Victoria, five months premature, was struggling for her life.

Ramonita made her way to the St. John Neumann shrine from St. Veronica's church without delay. She entered the display room that contains artifacts from the life of St. John Neumann. There she dropped to her knees and placed her palms on the marble step on which St. John Neumann collapsed and breathed his last breath. At the time, the body of St. John Neumann was temporarily preserved in this room because the main church was being refurbished. Ramonita gasped in desperation, "St. John, do something!"

From there she hurried over to Temple Hospital. The nurses would not grant Ramonita immediate permission to see Victoria because of her critical condition. Again Ramonita fell to her knees right in front of the door to the infant intensive care unit and prayed. Raising the relic of St. John Neumann in her hand in the direction of Victoria, Ramonita sighed in anguish, "St. John Neumann, let it be as if you are touching our baby."

Shortly thereafter, Ramonita was given a minute to go into the ICU and see her granddaughter. Victoria's undeveloped little body took Ramonita by surprise for an instant. So many tubes and contraptions were connected to her tiny limbs and torso that one could hardly make out a baby beneath it all.

Ramonita prayed a minute, thanked God that Victoria was baptized and then was ushered into the visitors' waiting room. Victoria remained at the hospital for one month.

At the end of that month Victoria was sent to St. Christopher's Hospital for heart surgery. She survived this ordeal. Today, at two years old, Victoria is a beautiful, loving, smiling, pleasant, affectionate and happy child. But the pre-natal neglect has taken its toll. As lovable as she is, Victoria is significantly behind in her physical and mental development.

But Ramonita and her family have every expectation that St. John Neumann, who saved their baby, will finish the work he has begun. If the saint could give Victoria the gift of life when all odds were against her, he can surely correct her present difficulties. ■

TOTALED

Senior week at the New Jersey shore resorts is synonymous with parties. Every year thousands of Philadelphia and New Jersey high school graduates swarm to the Jersey beaches the week after graduation. It almost seems like a peer-imposed rite of passage required for adulthood. But actually, senior week has more to do with beer than with maturity.

In the summer of 1973 Emmett McGraw was tuning up his red Volkswagen Beetle for the trip to the shore. At eighteen, he had just graduated from the prestigious St. Joseph's Prep School in Philadelphia. He loved sports. He played basketball and football and lifted weights. He excelled at golf. Emmett was a well-built, good-looking Irish redhead, popular with the girls. On top of that he was a nice kid, from a nice family. His mother, father, four brothers and one sister were a traditional Irish Catholic family active at Christ the King parish in Haddonfield, which was just around the corner from their house. John McGraw, the patriarch of the family, was always thankful to God that his children never had a problem with drugs or alcohol.

On Saturday, June 13th Emmett picked up his two friends Chris Fallon and Bob Fulton, long time neighborhood buddies. They were not the type to get into trouble. Their destination was a house in Sea Isle City, one of the resort towns on the Jersey coast. They were renting it with some other guys during senior week. They arrived in the afternoon and unpacked.

That night, Emmett, Chris and Bob jumped in the VW after dinner. Excitement overtook them as they anticipated the first of their big "nights on the town." They drove—radio blasting—to Mahoney's, a popular hot-spot for young people in Margate, a nearby shore point.

They were disappointed at the turnout for the beginning of senior week at this well-known "watering hole." It was an unusually slow night with few customers; "No action" as young people put it. Maybe it was the threatening rain clouds, maybe they were a day or two early. But the Haddonfield boys could enjoy themselves no matter what the situation.

The rage at the time was air hockey. Every tavern had a table. The winner had rights to the next game. Emmett loved this game and was good enough to hold a table all night, taking on all challengers. This night at Mahoney's was no different. Consecutive victories at the table left Emmett little time to drink beer. And since there were few girls patronizing Mahoney's that night, at least they could salvage some fun at the air hockey table.

After a while, even being an air hockey champ wore thin. It was 1:00 AM, and Emmett, Chris and Bob were ready to go back to Sea Isle City. It was raining slightly as they made their way through the empty parking lot to Emmett's Volkswagen. After a few turns they were cruising along the stretch of Landis Avenue, heading for Sea Isle City. Landis Avenue is a narrow coast road running between bogs of salt water inlets and tall grass. Occasionally a lone wooden house could be spotted sitting atop thin pilings above the bogs. Emmett had his window open and his arm resting on the door as the VW maintained a steady speed of forty miles per hour. They approached a bend. From this moment on, Emmett remembers nothing.

Coming from the opposite direction, five drunk teenagers in a late model Impala burst through the black silence of the night, crossed lanes at eighty miles per hour, and plowed head-long into the front left side of Emmett's VW. The Beetle was totally demolished. The impact of the heavy Impala literally turned the Volkswagen into a crushed up piece of tin foil. Bob Fulton, sitting in the back seat, was killed instantly. Chris Fallon, fully conscious during the entire accident, was thrown from the car. He suffered painful strains in his back muscles, but was otherwise alright.

When the screeching of tires and metal finally subsided, the Volkswagen door on Emmett's side was two hundred yards down the road, wrapped around the front of the Impala. Emmett was crushed into his vehicle beneath layers of twisted sheet metal that was once the red exterior of his VW. The rescue squad had to cut him free.

At the Cape May County Court House Hospital emergency room Emmett was already comatose. He had a broken collar bone, all of his front teeth were knocked out, he had serious glass lacerations of the left arm and he had suffered a severe blow to the left side of his head. While Emmett had no significant alcohol level in his bloodstream, neither did he register any vital signs. He was pronounced DOA.

The phone on John and Barbara McGraw's bedroom end table rang around 3:00 AM . The police sergeant's voice came over the phone, "Mr. McGraw, I'm sorry, your son Emmett has been in a serious car accident. Can you come down to the hospital and identify his body?" John and Barbara were physically sick during the hour and a half drive from Haddonfield to Cape May County Court House Hospital.

An anxious nurse greeted John and Barbara at the emergency room. She said, "Mr. McGraw, we found a heartbeat. Your son is not dead. But we don't have the facilities to treat him here." It was decided that Emmett would be transported that very day to the University of Pennsylvania Hospital, which has a renowned head injury unit.

Dr. Langfitt, the chief neurologist at the University of Pennsylvania Hospital, was awaiting Emmett's arrival. When Emmett was finally delivered to him, Dr. Langfitt sized up the situation. With all his knowledge and expertise, all he could do for Emmett was bore two holes in his skull to relieve the pressure on the brain. He was helpless in the face of Emmett's deep coma.

After extensive tests and analyses, Dr. Langfitt and his team of physicians gave the McGraws the prognosis: "Emmett will always be a vegetable. There is virtually no hope of recovery. His brain stem has been badly damaged by the severe blow to the head." The doctors recommended that the McGraws sign a form permitting the hospital to discontinue life support systems and make Emmett's organs available for donation. The McGraws refused to "pull the plug" on their son.

Steve McGraw, Emmett's older brother who had just graduated from Notre Dame University with honors, was not one to give up on his brother either. Over the next two months Steve visited Emmett at the hospital every day. With the doctor's tacit approval, he engaged Emmett in a daily program of sensory stimulation and physical therapy from 4:00 PM to 11:00 PM every day. He persevered despite Emmett's unresponsiveness.

The McGraws received a tremendous outpouring of support from their relatives and friends as well. Helen Pietz, a fellow parishioner from Christ the King parish, organized a nine week prayer novena for Emmett at the shrine of St. John Neumann. Two full bus loads of parishioners joined Helen and the McGraws every Wednesday evening for nine consecutive weeks, in prayers at the shrine for Emmett. Fr. Litz, C.SS.R., the director of the shrine at the time, would conclude each of these evenings with a Mass offered over the tomb of St. John Neumann, just for Emmett's intention.

John McGraw's business partner, Arthur Joseph, and his wife Judy also joined the parishioners each Wednesday night. Arthur joked with John, "This novena just has to work. It's the only Catholic novena I know of ever attended by a Jewish couple." (Art and Judy's son later went on to become a rabbi).

Helen Pietz also visited Emmett at the hospital within the first few days of his transfer. She gently touched a first class relic of St. John Neumann to his wounded head and prayed for a miracle.

Steve continued to spend his days at the hospital with his brother, and the prayers continued to ascend to heaven. The family rosary would be said in the car during every trip to the hospital. The family placed the relic and medal of St. John Neumann, given them by Helen, on Emmett every day they visited him. The McGraws always brought the relic home after each visit, though; they feared it might get lost in the laundry.

Over the next two months while Steve engaged Emmett in therapy and the family clung to God, Emmett contracted pneumonia and a staph infection, and his deep dormition persisted. The doctors again predicted he would not survive these setbacks.

Although there was no clear turning point in Emmett's condition, on Saturday, August 15, the Feast of Our Lady's Assumption and two months after the accident, a ray of hope surfaced. A bus load of Christ the King parishioners were attending Mass for the Holy Day at the St. John Neumann shrine with the McGraws. As they were leaving the chapel after Mass, Steve met them at the entrance. He had just been with Emmett at the University of Pennsylvania Hospital. He rushed up the church steps into the Haddonfield contingent. "Emmett is beginning to move, as if he is about to come out of the coma," he blurted out with excitement. The excitement was contagious. It sparked new hope and faith as they all gave thanks to God.

Steve, who became the family activist in his brother's recovery, was convinced that Emmett could be rehabilitated. He believed from the very beginning that his brother's recovery was possible, but that it would be a long process, occurring inch by inch, day by day.

Despite the positive signs, Emmett still could not see or talk. He had virtually no motor control. He had lost eighty pounds. His legs would periodically go into trembling seizures. But he was slowly coming out of his coma. Emmett's team of ten doctors were willing to transfer him to a rehabilitation center, but they advised the McGraws not to get their hopes up because "Emmett would never walk again." John McGraw angrily retorted, "Emmett will walk and talk and see. We are asking God for one-hundred percent, why should you aim for less?"

Emmett received speech, occupational and physical therapy at the rehabilitation center. Steve supplemented each day with his own eight hour routine with Emmett, but Steve felt strongly that the family could give Emmett more attention at home. John and Barbara hesitantly agreed. Emmett came home in November. He was still only half-awake; he looked and acted like someone who was both crippled and mentally handicapped.

Steve worked with his brother fifteen hours a day and the rest of the family contributed selflessly as well. The living room became Emmett's physical therapy gymnasium. The prayers continued to rise to heaven from

Haddonfield, Fifth and Girard and elsewhere. Emmett continued to improve, "inch by inch, day by day" as Steve predicted.

The rest of the story is history. Emmett went on to walk, talk, and see. Today he has eighty-five percent of his physical capacities and one hundred percent of his mental capacities. He attended college and has held jobs in Ft. Lauderdale, New York City, Myrtle Beach and Switzerland. Today Emmett works at the Eldorado Casino in Reno. He derives great pleasure from traveling, but his roots are still in Haddonfield.

Emmett's story has since received wide acclaim. A chronicle of the McGraw saga was written in novel form by Steve and published under the title *Totaled* by William Marrow and Company. *Readers Digest* picked up the story and published it in its condensed versions in the United States, Canada, Japan, Italy, Norway and Australia. *Guideposts* magazine also covered Emmett's comeback in its monthly periodical, which was circulated in both the United States and Korea.

Emmett, Steve and the family have been interviewed on several television talk shows as well. Steve battled with Hollywood producers for 10 years over a made-for-TV movie script he wrote. In frustration he finally threw in the towel. CBS will be airing "their version" of Emmett's story in a soon-to-be-released movie entitled *Miles From Nowhere*.* Steve was very disappointed in the final version of the script. Most references to God and prayer had been subtracted from his original draft, as well as other important details. Steve said to Barbara regarding the movie, "Mom, when you see it, you won't even recognize the story."

But the McGraws have not subtracted God from their final version. When John McGraw died peacefully at home in early July 1991 at seventy, many of the same parishioners from Christ the King Church who had been so supportive 18 years before came to pay their respects at the wake. At the funeral home the McGraw family greeted one and all, and among them was Helen Pietz.

When Helen reached the family to offer her condolences, Emmett smiled and reached inside his shirt. He pulled out a chain which was around his neck. Attached to the chain was the relic and medal of St. John Neumann that Helen had given to his family in the days immediately following his accident. Emmett has worn it ever since.

Barbara remarked to Helen, "It baffles me how Emmett has still hung onto that medal all this time. He is so prone to lose things: watches, wallets, jewelry, especially since he travels all over the world. It's a mystery to me."

The mystery brought tears to Helen's eyes.   ■

* The movie was aired Tuesday, January 7, 1992.

Emmett McGraw (right) of Haddonfield, New Jersey pictured in 1991
with his brother Steve and his sister-in-law Nancy. Emmett was given up
for dead in 1973.

II

CHILDREN: HIS FAVORITES

In life, St. John Neumann loved children. Incidents of his kindnesses and affection for them are plentiful in his biographies. Neumann himself confessed more than once that he found the greatest satisfaction in teaching children the Catholic faith. He did this even as a bishop, and children always found him attractive and approachable. After all, they were his favorites.

The saint's love for children has survived his death. He continues to work his most extraordinary prodigies for sick children. Experience has proved that St. John Neumann is still befriending children from heaven and sending his fatherly protection, as the next few stories relate.

A MOTHER'S INTUITION

When Marie Milano was growing up in the row homes on Germantown Avenue between Second and Third Streets in the 1930's and 1940's, life was a lot simpler. Her parents didn't worry about Marie and her brothers when they walked the few blocks to St. Peter's school. In fact, anyone could stroll along Girard Avenue at any time of the day without the least bit of fear. Such was Philadelphia during those years.

Some Philadelphians were hoping that the "City of Brotherly Love" might be favored with another grace in the ensuing decades as well. Fr. Waible, the Redemptorist priest from the Bishop John Neumann shrine was the promoter of John Neumann's cause for sainthood. He had already been named "Venerable," a term which officially recognizes the heroic virtue of his life. The next step which Fr. Waible was pressing for was the rank of "Blessed."

So an awareness of the life of Bishop John Neumann was part and parcel of Marie Milano's Catholic education at St. Peter's parish school at Fifth and Girard. The Redemptorist priests made sure of that. As a young girl Marie remembers being quite open to devotion to John Neumann. In fact on one occasion Fr. Waible himself took notice of Marie's artistic talent and asked her to develop some sketches for possible use for a new holy card of Bishop Neumann. When she drew those sketches in her early teens, Marie had no conception of how largely John Neumann would factor in her later life.

This was Marie's childhood association with the future saint and his shrine. In fact, Marie eventually went on to marry her husband, Robert Sr., at St. Peter's as well. They had six beautiful children: Marie, Cheryl, Kenneth, Robert Jr., Linda and Michelle, all of whom went on to attend St. Peter's school like their mother.

In 1963, the efforts of Fr. Waible and his co-workers on behalf of their Redemptorist brother John Neumann, paid off. Pope Paul VI declared him blessed that year. Everyone at St. Peter's parish rejoiced.

Marie's oldest daughter was in the first grade then. She was chosen to carry some of Blessed John Neumann's artifacts in the grand procession during the Triduum of ceremonies at St. Peter's marking this great pronouncement by Pope Paul VI. The priests gave her a gold case containing a first class relic of John Neumann for her participation in the ceremonies. A pious token? Perhaps. But how priceless that relic would become to the family in future years.

Around this time their sixth child was born. She was a blond-haired, blue-eyed little darling named Michelle. At the encouragement of Sister Timothy, a teacher at St. Peter's school, Marie brought her newborn infant to the convent and consecrated her to the Blessed Virgin Mary. Michelle was the only one of her six children to receive this grace.

Within a year or two the Milanos moved to York Street, near Memphis Street in the Port Richmond area of Philadelphia. They became members of St. Ann's parish. They missed the activity at the Neumann shrine, but they were quite content in their new home. They had no idea when they moved that York Street would be the setting of some profoundly dramatic events which would leave a lasting imprint on their family life.

It was May 1, 1966, Kenny's birthday. Marie took her son to a toy store on Kensington Avenue to get him some birthday gifts. Little Michelle, three years old at the time, was very attached to her mother. She was made to stay at home this time, so she began to cry.

Robert Sr. could not pacify his daughter Michelle after his wife and Kenny left for their shopping trip. Beside himself with frustration he called his two older daughters Marie, twelve, and Cheryl, ten. "Marie and Cheryl, please take Michelle down to the candy store on the corner. Michelle, here is a nickel, get whatever you want," instructed Robert. Michelle's tears halted.

Michelle tagged along with Marie and Cheryl as they gathered some of their neighborhood friends for their little pilgrimage to the candy store. Still sulking, Michelle fell a few paces behind the girls, but stayed with them. No way would she miss this treat.

At approximately 1:15 PM while Marie and Kenny were foraging through the toy store on Kensington Avenue, Marie was seized by a terrible grip of fear. It came on instantaneously and coursed through her body like high voltage electricity. She knew with certainty that something was gravely wrong at home. She told Kenny that they would come back for the remainder of his gifts the next day, but that they had to get back home immediately. They paid for their merchandise and began the walk home. Kenny could hardly keep up with his mother.

As they turned up York Street about three blocks from their house Marie was almost running. She looked up and saw a crowd of people gathered on the street in her neighborhood. Marie hoped that it was just the familiar gang of kids who often hang out at the corner near the candy store. She didn't realize it, but she was squeezing Kenny's hand tighter and tighter.

Then Marie's heart forced its way to her throat. She spotted a car up on the sidewalk near her house. Marie dropped her shopping bags, clenched Kenny's hand with a vice-grip, and broke into a full sprint.

As they raced down York Street, the streetlight poles whizzed by surrealistically. A block from the house, a girl of about twelve was clinging to one of the streetlight poles. She was hysterical. It was Betty Ann, one of Cheryl's and Marie's friends. Without breaking stride Marie yelled out to Betty Ann, "Which one of my children is it?" Call it a mother's intuition; call it what you will, Marie was sure it was one of hers.

"Michelle," answered Betty Ann, choking back sobs. Within seconds Marie reached the car, broke through the crowd and saw her little Michelle lying on the pavement crying, still conscious.

Michelle looked at her mother with tears in her eyes and struggled to call her. "Mommy," she cried. As she did so she attempted to reach her arms out to her mother, but only her right arm extended. Her left arm fell limp at her side.

The car that was on the sidewalk had veered out of control and jumped the curb. By the time it came to a stop, the front fender had crashed through a wooden fence which ran along side the neighbor's home on York Street. Michelle had been caught between the fender and the fence. On impact the fence broke, and the jagged wood of the fence severed Michelle's left arm.

When Michelle's older sister went to pick her up, Michelle's severed arm started to slip through the sleeve of her light-weight jacket. When Marie saw this she too became hysterical. Her husband had to pull her back so that she would not touch Michelle, and perhaps further damage her arm. Helplessness and extreme frustration strained everyones' emotions as they waited those few moments, which seemed like decades, for the ambulance to arrive.

Michelle was rushed to the emergency room of St. Mary's Hospital. The doctors assessed her injuries: she had sustained a fractured skull, and her left arm was completely severed, except for a small strip of skin. Dr. Blaker, the orthopedic surgeon on call at the time, initiated emergency surgery on Michelle's arm immediately. He attempted to re-attach and reconstruct the bones, muscles, nerves, vessels and arteries of her left arm.

When Michelle emerged from six hours of intensive surgery, her arm and shoulder were completely encased in a plaster cast, save the tips of her fingers. Dr. Blaker explained to Marie after the procedure that he expected to amputate her daughter's arm in three or four days. The bones, nerves, muscles, vessels—everything—had been irreparably damaged.

Marie spent those four days in the hospital with her daughter. Every day she blessed Michelle's arm and head with the first class relic of St. John

Neumann her daughter had received three years before from the priests at St. Peter's on the occasion of John Neumann's beatification.

At the end of the four day period Dr. Blaker was surprised to discover warmth in Michelle's fingers. He now thought that the arm could be saved, but she would never have use of it. Michelle had also survived the fractured skull with no brain damage.

When Michelle came home from the hospital and the cast was removed, she had a wrist drop—her hand hung at her side from the wrist. Marie continued to bless her daughter's arm and wrist with the relic. She offered prayers many times per day to John Neumann. Marie also employed Michelle in a little form of physical therapy that she devised herself: she would carefully close Michelle's left hand over a small rubber ball and gently and repeatedly squeeze it. The doctor said this was useless. Michelle had no hope of using her left arm again. When Michelle went to bed at night, the relic of St. John Neumann would go with her.

Every week Michelle reported to Dr. Blaker at the orthopedic clinic for observation. On their eighth visit Marie broke the news to Dr. Blaker, "Doctor, Michelle can control her left arm and hand."

Dr. Blaker stood up, left the patient he was attending at the moment and dashed over to Michelle.

"Impossible," he retorted.

He barked out several commands to Michelle to move her left arm and hand:

"Straight out! Straight up! Down! Now, straight out again!"

Michelle readily responded to each command with fluid, controlled movements of her hand and arm.

"This is miraculous! I never thought she would use that arm or hand again," confessed Dr. Blaker.

Michelle went on to graduate from Hallahan High School. She became a typist and medical secretary, although she must use an electric typewriter. She can do everything with her left arm that she can do with her right arm, although the left arm is a little weaker.

Today she is twenty-eight, married and a mother of three children, whom she carries in her left arm. She is happily living and working in Wildwood, New Jersey, with her husband and family. Of course, her children have been baptized at the Neumann shrine.

Michelle says that ever since her recovery she has had no fear. She feels that St. John Neumann is close to her, protecting her.

Marie still lives in the same house on York Street. When she was relating the details of this story to the author, Marie was minding her two granddaughters (Michelle's daughter Amy, eight, and Cheryl's daughter,

Tonya, eleven) who overheard her. They pleaded with Marie, "Grandmom, will you take us to see St. John Neumann? Please."

At the shrine the girls were fascinated and bubbled over with questions. "Grandmom, is he the one that made mommy all better?" asked Amy.

"Yes, Amy, he certainly is," said Marie.

A GIFT FOR THE TWINS

Sharon and Michael O'Brien of the Northwood section of Northeast Philadelphia became the proud young parents of twin boys, Daniel and Matthew, in February of 1988. When the boys came home from the hospital they both grew rapidly. But with their growth surfaced an apparent problem. At the ten month mark Daniel was already walking. But walking seemed a virtual impossibility for Matthew, much to his frustration. He would stand, gain his balance for a moment, take a step and fall instantly. Sharon and Mike noticed at this time that Matthew developed a pronounced outward curvature in his left leg and knee, and his foot seemed to take a "C" shape.

Mike and Sharon took Matthew to a specialist at St. Christopher's Hospital. The doctor's examination confirmed the fact that Matthew had the combined orthopedic abnormalities called tibial torsion and metatarsal abduction. In layman's terms this means that Matthew was severely pigeon-toed in both feet, and that his legs, when not held down, would spontaneously contract into a yoga position and spring "like rubber bands" up against his belly.

The specialist said that after breaking, resetting, casting and baring Matthew's legs, it could take up to ten years of wearing special shoes and braces for Matthew to walk. Even after this lengthy treatment, the doctor was sure that the problem would never go away completely. He noted that there was a significant possibility that the procedure would be unsuccessful, even if the treatment was administered properly, because Matthew had already grown so much in ten months. The doctor explained that corrective therapy of this sort is normally commenced immediately at birth if it is to be successful. At any rate he would prescribe special orthopedic shoes for Matthew and recommended that they all hope for the best.

Sharon and Mike returned home stricken with sadness and worry. They didn't know what was best for their son. They agonized over the options. In the meantime they purchased the special shoes and worked with Matthew endlessly.

Matthew gave it his very best. At his parents' encouragement he would lift himself to his feet, holding onto the living room sofa. Sharon and Mike would fill themselves with false hopes and applaud vigorously, hoping that their enthusiasm would give Matthew confidence. He would let go of his support, take an unsteady step or two, then his foot would flip into a curve and he would fall into the arms of his parents.

"Excellent, Matthew!" Sharon would shout, fighting back tears so as not to let her son experience failure.

Meanwhile Daniel progressed from walking to running and getting on his own two feet without the aid of a stationary object to assist him. Matthew would have to resort to crawling, dragging his legs underneath himself in order to play and keep up with his brother.

This was the state of affairs at the O'Brien home on that Friday morning in January, 1989 when Mr. and Mrs. O'Brien (Mike's parents) came to visit their grandsons. Mike was at work that day. Mr. and Mrs. O'Brien told Sharon they had a gift for the boys. To the probable disappointment of the boys, their grandparents produced a relic of St. John Neumann; they would have much preferred toys or candy.

Mr. O'Brien touched the relic to Matthew's legs, knees, and feet. Sharon and the grandparents prayed for the saint's intercession. At this point Sharon was open to anything. The mere act of praying gave her relief. Mr. and Mrs. O'Brien finished their coffee and were on their way.

When Mike arrived home from work that afternoon his wife left for her job. Daniel greeted him as usual, running toward him with arms outstretched, wanting to be picked up. But this day, scampering right behind him on his own two feet was Matthew. He had just crossed the length of the house with no assistance to greet his father.

Mike was thrilled, but he was also exhausted after a long week. He knew nothing of his parent's visit that day, so he credited Matthew's improvement to the special shoes. Mike gathered up Matthew and Daniel in his arms and kissed them. He began to prepare the boys' bottles for dinner. In his fatigue and preoccupation with his duties the matter slipped his mind.

Saturday morning came and Sharon was off to work again. Because Mike and Sharon both work, they run a tight schedule at times. Sharon already had the boys dressed and their morning bottles warmed. Mike fed the boys their milk and gulped a few mouthfuls of cereal and coffee himself. As he was taking the empty bottles from the boys, he thought that he would give Matthew's feet a break and remove his orthopedic shoes.

When he set Matthew down on the kitchen floor, to his astonishment, Matthew planted both feet firmly and flatly on the floor and stood erect and independently. Mike examined his legs and feet and could no longer notice the "C" shape in them. Matthew's face beamed with pride as he scurried into the living room to join his brother at play.

Mike recalls that at that very moment the phone rang and he learned of Bishop Neumann's visit to his home the day before.

The boys are three years old now. Since the day of the blessing Matthew's right and left legs are straight and his right foot is straight. There remains only a slight slant in his left foot. He has also worn normal shoes for the past two years.

According to Sharon, Matthew is now a terror. He jumps off chairs, runs into furniture and appliances, and gets into everything.

Mike and Sharon sincerely believe that this gift was given to them through the intercession of St. John Neumann. It has inspired a renewed devotion to prayer and the sacraments in the whole family, and a great appreciation for the fatherly concern of the wonder-worker of Philadelphia.

LADY LIBERTY'S BIRTHDAY

On Wednesday, June 29, 1977 John and Rose Pascale of Neptune, New Jersey admitted their four-year-old son Paul to the Jersey Shore Medical Center. He was suffering from complications of influenza. His condition took a quick turn for the worse and soon little Paul was rapidly falling into a coma. He was diagnosed as having meningitis, which instigated the onset of encephalitis. The Pascales were devastated. They had to muster all their interior strength just to keep themselves from collapsing into a paralysis of fear. The night was long and sleepless.

The next morning, in the Medical Center lobby, a woman who identified herself as a hospital switchboard operator approached the Pascales directly.

"I hear that there is a sick boy in the hospital," she said to Rose. At the same time this stranger stuffed a card into Rose's hand.

"Pray to him. He is a new saint and is not too busy yet," she exhorted.

She left as quickly as she had come.

Within minutes John and Rose were hustling to their car. Paul was being transferred to another hospital in an ambulance. John stayed right on the ambulance's tail as it weaved through traffic.

At this point Rose was recollected enough to unfold her fist and open up the card that was thrust into her hand in the lobby moments before.

It was a prayer card to St. John Neumann. Rose recited the prayer aloud. When she came to the phrase, "God will give us the grace to accept His holy will," John and Rose burst into tears. At that instant they knew in their hearts that their son Paul would die. Yet at the same time a mysterious peace came over them.

When they arrived at the hospital Paul was ushered right in for tests. His EEG was flat, registering total brain death. The EEG was repeated the next day with the same results.

"In this case the Lord healed my boy perfectly, taking Paul to Himself," mused Rose. She was amazed at her own attitude of interior resignation.

She and John were healed also. They were granted a tremendous grace of peace and inner strength throughout their trying bereavement. After Paul's death, during the funeral arrangements and wake and Mass, and in fact for a full two weeks after, this peace stayed with them. Their many relatives and friends who supported them through this ordeal were surprised at their composure and inner calmness. There were tears of course, but no medication, no uncontrollable grief or hysteria.

John and Rose didn't know what to make of the switchboard operator they met in the lobby of the Jersey Shore Medical Center. But they did know that the little prayer to St. John Neumann turned an unbearable tragedy into a bearable trial. Before they received that prayer card from her they had never heard of St. John Neumann.

★ ★ ★ ★ ★ ★ ★

Seven years later the Pascales were shocked again. In January of 1985 their youngest son, five-year-old Joseph, appeared to have the symptoms of bacterial meningitis. The family was stricken with terror and disbelief. The chances of two such cases in the same family were highly improbable. The outcome of Paul's bout with the disease came flooding to the forefront of Rose's and John's memory with blistering clarity.

Within a year and a half, in early July, 1986, Joseph developed the same neurological signs as his deceased brother. On July 3 he slipped into a coma and was admitted to the Jersey Shore Medical Center. When Rose and Bob entered the Medical Center, the sights, sounds and smells caused them to grow weak-kneed, so much did these images recall in their minds the tragic events of the summer of 1977.

A spinal tap was performed on Joseph. Rose's and John's worst fears were realized. The diagnosis was definite — Joseph had meningitis. Rose remembers the date clearly because it was the night that all of the festivities were being conducted around Ellis Island for the "birthday" of Lady Liberty.

President Reagan and his entourage were the guests of honor at the grand party which included fireworks, a laser light show, hundreds of boats in the harbor and squads of air force jets overhead. Lady Liberty was 100 years old and the country was experiencing a resurgence of patriotism at the time.

There were also threats that the party would be thwarted by international terrorism. Rumors of an attack by Gadhafi were running strong. The United States military was taking every precaution, including closing the airways in a large radius around Ellis Island. Security was at a maximum. As can be imagined at an affair like this, automobile traffic was immobilized.

The Pascales were not in a partying mood that night. The doctors at the South Jersey Medical Center wanted to transfer Joseph to New York Hospital by helicopter, where they had the proper expertise and facilities to attempt to treat him. It was an extreme emergency, a matter of life and death.

The officials at the Jersey Shore Medical Center were trying desperately to arrange for a passage through the secure airspace. They even attempted to reach the governor to see if an emergency provision could be made. All efforts were futile. The airways were closed. Joseph would not have the benefit that night of the type of specialized care his condition required.

Rose became angry at God. She stormed through the corridors of the South Jersey Medical Center crying out to God in disbelief and despair. "Why, after taking my first son Paul, do you now deprive my Joseph of what he needs on the most critical night of his life?" she shouted.

The staff at the South Jersey Medical Center worked with Joseph diligently with all the resources at their disposal. Many relatives, friends and clergy came to pray with the Pascales at the Medical center. Waiting and praying in the hall outside Joseph's room, everyone prepared for the worst. All wondered if Rose would recover from a second such devastating blow.

But God's grace was beginning to touch Rose. She offered a second prayer — a mother's prayer, as only a mother can do, "Lord, if it is Your will that Joseph get better this time, it means that You have a plan for him; if not, take him now. We can't live in fear for the rest of our lives." She cried all night.

At some point in the night the Pascales' parish priest arrived to comfort the family. Fr. Eugene Roberts anointed Joseph and blessed him with a first class relic of St. John Neumann. Upon departing he left the relic on Joseph's pillow.

Later, the family was permitted to enter Joseph's room for a while. They surrounded his bed and prayed the rosary. Rose noticed that his foot moved. A flash of hope lighted up her heart.

The next morning, by the time Joseph was on his way to New York Hospital he was already improving. Within twelve days Joseph recovered. He had survived two terrible insults to his brain caused by the encephalitis related to the meningitis.

Today Joseph has a normal IQ, plays sports and is a healthy, happy child. His EEG is still abnormal and he is being weaned off medication that was prescribed merely for precautionary purposes. Joseph also has a little difficulty processing information. But these obstacles in no way prevent him from enjoying a happy, normal, productive life, nor will they in the future.

Joseph understands that he has a purpose in life. His mother confided to him the prayer she prayed that night of July 3, 1986. Rose and John speak often to Joseph about St. John Neumann. Rose was saying that just the other night Joseph told her, "Mom, I love St. John Neumann. He's my friend."

In the wake of all these happenings, the Pascales and their loved ones have had a great turn-around in their personal faith lives. They can recall the doctors using the word "miracle" several times in regard to Joseph's case.

Rose and John now keep that relic of St. John Neumann in the kitchen of their home. Whenever family members are sick, even with a common cold, they are blessed with the relic.

After they had a chance to recover, Rose and John went back to the Jersey Shore Medical Center to see if they could track down the switchboard operator who first introduced them to St. John Neumann in 1977. They were disappointed that they could not locate her. No one in the hospital could identify such a woman based on Rose's and John's description. Nine years had passed since their strange encounter in the lobby; she could be anywhere now. But the Pascales are grateful to her nonetheless. ∎

ANOTHER BLESSING
FOR HADDONFIELD

Born two years after Emmett McGraw, Jim Carmody was raised in the same town and attended the same church as Emmett. Jim was the oldest son of James and Margaret Carmody, who also had three other children: Elaine, Gary and Stephen.

From a very early age, Jim proved to be very athletically inclined. He harbored a secret desire to eventually become a professional athlete and he seemed to have the potential talent for it too.

When Jim was ten years old his parents permitted him to join the Haddonfield midget football team. It was 1966 (seven years before Emmett's accident) and Jim was having an excellent game one colorful, crisp, sunny autumn Saturday. During this, his first season, Jim excelled in each game and was known for his robust endurance and hard hitting.

Suddenly, Jim's coach caught sight of him out on the field of play, raising his hand and indicating that he wanted to come out of the game. The coach was astonished, given Jim's rugged physique. Reaching the sidelines, Jim took off his helmet. He was white, weak and unsteady. He complained of a headache. The head coach assisted Jim to the bench. The coaching staff thought that he was just shaken up, as happens often in football, and that their little star would be back in play shortly. "Shake it off, Jimmy," they groused, as they patted his backside and went back to the sidelines to observe play.

One of the spectators at the game was a doctor. He too had a son playing for Haddonfield. He walked over to the bench and examined Jim. The doctor quickly informed the coaching staff that "something was seriously wrong" with Jim. An ambulance was called immediately and Jim was taken to Our Lady of Lourdes Hospital in Camden, New Jersey.

When Margaret Carmody arrived at the hospital she found her son in the emergency room, lying on a stretcher. The physician in the emergency room approached her and said, "Don't worry Mrs. Carmody, Jim is fine. He can go home with you in about twenty minutes." "Thank God," thought Margaret, "the worry is over."

As Margaret was patiently waiting those few minutes for Jim, Dr. Rushton, a fellow parishioner of Christ the King Parish in Haddonfield, came walking through the emergency room. Dr. Rushton at the time was a member of the Lourdes Hospital staff and a highly respected neurosurgeon. He had just finished a long shift and was on his way home, looking a bit tired.

"Hello, Margaret. What brings you here?" he said to Mrs. Carmody.

"My son was injured in a football game, but apparently he is fine now. I'm waiting to take him home," she replied.

Out of kindness Dr. Rushton stopped to look at Jim. His face turned serious. Within moments he saw how bad Jim really was.

He turned to Margaret and said gently, "Your boy is very ill." Margaret stood up in confusion and mumbled some half-hearted objections, but Dr. Rushton was already ordering Jim to be taken up to surgery for a spinal tap. Despite his fatigue, he put all of his medical sagacity at the Carmodys service and took personal charge of Jim's case.

As Dr. Rushton suspected, the spinal tap revealed that there was blood in the spinal cord, meaning that Jim was hemorrhaging from the brain. Jim, it seemed, had an unknown malformation in his brain that was ruptured from contact during the football game.

Jim quickly lapsed into a coma. James and Margaret took up residence in the hospital, preparing for a long vigil of anguish. Since Margaret's parents lived with her, the other children were in good hands, which was one less worry.

Hour by hour the Carmodys were given a status report: it was touch and go. The doctors didn't think that Jim would make it. He was not responding to any treatment and remained in a deep coma. Margaret and James were advised to "get themselves ready for the worst." Dr. Rushton did not expect Jim to recover, but he kept his prediction to himself. But one nurse caring for Jim couldn't do the same. Thinking that she was helping the Carmodys prepare for the inevitable she said to Margaret, "It would be better if he died, because if he lives he will be a vegetable."

The situation seemed precarious and fear began to overshadow the Carmodys. They had just dropped their healthy, vibrant son off to play a little football, and hours later he was hanging at death's doorstep. They began to wonder if this just wasn't all a bad dream, and that they would soon wake up.

The vigil of anguish and uncertainty persisted for days. Jim was still in a coma teetering between life and death. Margaret and James were at the hospital through it all. Then, at the seven day mark, Margaret received a phone call at the hospital. It seemed to come out of the blue. Helen Pietz, a person Margaret never met but knew of from Christ the King parish, was on the line. By now, half of Haddonfield was aware of the unfortunate accident involving Jim Carmody.

Helen: Mrs. Carmody? This is Helen Pietz.

Margaret: Yes, Helen, I know of you. What do you want?

Helen: I heard about Jim, and I was wondering if you would like Fr. Litz from the Neumann shrine to come to Lourdes Hospital and bless him?

Margaret: Sure Helen, we can use all the prayers we can get, at this point!

Helen: Good, Margaret. Then we'll see you tonight.

Although Margaret knew nothing of John Neumann at the time, she was very open to her Catholic faith and also in great need.

That night, at about 10:00 PM Fr. Litz, the Redemptorist priest who directed the Neumann shrine, entered Jim's room with Helen. Margaret and James quietly greeted them. The introductions were terse and cordial; everyone knew the seriousness of the situation.

Fr. Litz lead them in the recitation of some prayers, and then Jim was blessed with a first class relic of then Blessed John Neumann. The entire visit was a short one. Fr. Litz and Helen completed their mission and were on their way. Sincere thanks was all the Carmodys could offer them.

At 11:00 PM Margaret and James left Jim's room and went downstairs to the visitors' waiting room for a few hours sleep. They were emotionally exhausted, and as Margaret was drifting off to sleep she was deeply discouraged. She was hoping for a miracle, and the prayers and blessing seemed to have little effect on her son's comatose body.

The next morning, when James and Margaret went up to their son's room, they were taken totally off guard. Jim was sitting up in bed, fully conscious, devouring a full breakfast.

"What happened!" exclaimed Margaret and Jim.

"Hi mom. Hi dad," said Jim between mouthfuls.

James and Margaret ran over to their son and covered him with hugs and kisses. They were crying with joy. Little Jim just wanted to eat his breakfast.

Jim continued to progress and was home in another week. The Carmodys pressed Dr. Rushton for an explanation and he commented that, "Some things just can't be explained. It was certainly something different than medicine that brought about Jim's recovery."

The nurse who had given no hope to Jim caught the Carmodys in the corridor and apologized. She was so happy to see this turn of events.

Today Jim is thirty-five years old, married with two children, is a certified, licensed optician and a very happy and healthy man. He believes his recovery was a miracle, and even when he was ten he felt that he was spared because there is a purpose to his life. Jim is not permitted to play sports for his own safety, and the acceptance of this limitation by a young man who once had unbounded confidence in his physical capacities is an amazing transformation in itself.

The entire family credits Jim's recovery to St. John Neumann, and they have a greater faith in God and a deep devotion to the Church as a result of their experience. Margaret says that the events affected all who witnessed or heard of them: "Believers were strengthened in their faith, and unbelievers wondered at the mystery of it all." ∎

AN EARLY CHRISTMAS IN ROXBOROUGH

Roxborough is a small, blue-collar community along the banks of the Schuylkill River just inside the western limits of the City of Philadelphia. The row homes of Roxborough are inhabited by frank, down-to-earth folks who are also very patriotic and very neighborly. In this stable community people still know their neighbors. In the summer evenings they sit on each other's front steps and porches and sip beer and iced tea together and talk about sports, politics, the other neighbors and the Mayor of Philadelphia. Should an emergency ever arise, you could be sure that the neighbors would be the first to rally around those in difficulty. Roxborough is "bedrock America" and proud of it.

Mike Kost grew up in this traditional patch of Philadelphia on Evergreen Avenue. His parish was St. Josaphat. In 1965, when he was six years old his mother noticed a lump on his neck. It was soon diagnosed as cancer – non-Hodgkins lymphoma. The oncologists at Children's Hospital in Philadelphia said that Mike's cancer was in stage four. In the staging system in medicine, one indicates the best chance of recovery and four indicates the worst prognosis.

When Mike's parents were informed that the cancer had spread to the liver and metastasized around one of his vertebra as well, they were crushed. His team of physicians and surgeons at Children's Hospital, which included former Surgeon General C. Everet Koop, told Mr. and Mrs. Kost that nothing could be done for Mike; he would be dead before Christmas. They prescribed what is now considered a very primitive form of chemo-and radiation therapy, as a token treatment for a hopeless case. Mike's parents decided to make the best of what little time they had left, so they decided to celebrate Christmas for him early that year.

Christmas in Roxborough is made up of all the traditional stuff that evokes yuletide cheer — row homes lined with strings of lights and boughs of holly, candles in the windows, carols blasting through the streets from the corner drug store, good food, family and friends. The Kosts used to love this season, but this year nothing could rouse them from their depression. In fact, Christmas shopping was a most painful chore. Each gift they purchased and wrapped for Mike was a searing reminder that it would be the last.

But the Kosts were not content to let the token treatment prescribed at Children's Hospital suffice. They began some treatment of their own for their son. Hearing about John Neumann (Venerable at the time) from some nurses at Roxborough Hospital, the Kosts began to make visits to the shrine on Sundays about twice a month. Mike was blessed with the first class relic by the priests at the shrine. His parents procured their own first class relic also and used it to bless Mike daily.

Over the next three years, although Mike had frequent bouts with his sickness and was under the care of the Children's Hospital Oncology unit, he improved. His bi-monthly "treatments" at the shrine and his daily "doses" of blessings with the relic continued too.

Mike became well enough to attend grade school at St. Josaphat's and his health progressed to the point where his association with Children's Hospital was no longer necessary. In 1970 he underwent an extensive, two-day examination for cancer. Not a trace of it could be found anywhere in his body. The doctors were heard using the words "living miracle," and they said that there was no medical reason why Mike should be alive.

Mike went on to graduate from Roman Catholic High School. During his years at Roman, he grew in his appreciation of St. John Neumann. During those years he would often walk or take a bus from the high school on Vine Street up to Fifth and Girard and visit the shrine after school.

In 1977 a contingent of priests, religious and lay people from the Philadelphia area chartered a jet to Rome for John Neumann's canonization ceremonies. With the money Mike saved from working at a local supermarket he joined this group. His traveling companion was a priest who was a good friend of the family.

In Rome Mike met Michael Flanigan. Flanigan was another young Philadelphia man whose recovery from a fatal disease had no medical explanation. He had osteosarcoma of the leg and lung, and he and his loved ones prayed to St. John Neumann for help. Flanigan's recovery was accepted as one of the miracles for Neumann's canonization. Together in this climate of faith, the two young men relished the excitement of the ceremonies, the thrill of Rome and the sharing of their personal testimonies of the power of Bishop Neumann's intercession. Mike Kost remembers it as one of the most glorious moments of his life.

In fact, Mike's recovery was also being reviewed by a cardinal in Rome as the fourth miracle for John Neumann's cause. But at the last minute, Pope Paul VI dispensed the requirement of the fourth miracle for Neumann's canonization. Consequently, the review of Kost's case became unnecessary and was dropped by the Congregation for the Causes of Saints.

Mike is thirty-two years old today. He is a happy husband and father of three children. He lives with his family in Blue Bell, Pennsylvania. As might be expected, Mike chose a career in the medical profession. He still has his parent's relic and wears a medal of the saint. Every night he prays the novena prayers to Saint John Neumann.

Mike has been subject to two thorough physical examinations annually until he was twenty-five, and a yearly examination since then. His body remains cancer-free. ∎

THE TAFFY AND THE SAINT

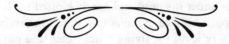

It was late summer 1961, and Eleanor Scholz was in the kitchen of her home in the Wissynoming section of Northeast Philadelphia. She was preparing dinner, and her husband Frank would be home from work soon. At 6:00 PM each night Eleanor and Frank would sit down for a family meal with their sons Mark, eight, Frank Jr., seven, and David, six. The routine was the same every evening, and Eleanor had grown comfortable and content with the stability of her quiet family life.

As Eleanor was milling around the kitchen, she could hear her sons and their friends outside in the backyard. They were running, jumping, shouting and playing with the boundless energy of youngsters. As she washed the vegetables in the kitchen sink she looked out the window. All the neighborhood kids were in her yard, including the little girl from next door. "There she is with that taffy again. Her mother keeps telling her she will get hurt running with it in her mouth, but she doesn't listen," reflected Eleanor to herself.

Eleanor's thoughts drifted away from the little girl next door and she began to ponder the simplicity and dignity of motherhood. She wondered if her own mother felt this way when she was young, as she fulfilled the routine chores of daily life as a middle class, suburban mother and housewife. It all seemed so pedestrian and archaic, and at the same time so nostalgic, fulfilling and enriching. One thing was for sure, thought Eleanor, as she smiled to herself, "I love it, and I wouldn't give it up for the world."

Then came the scream that pierced her daydream. Her son David came running into the house crying uncontrollably with his hands over his left eye. Blood was dripping between his fingers. "Mommy, Mommy! My eye, my eye!" he yelled repeatedly.

Eleanor felt the strength drain from her body. Panic began to squeeze her like a "body vice." A queasiness gripped her stomach. She fought it. She had to remain rational for her son's sake.

She ran over to David, swept him up in her arms and laid him down on the couch. Eleanor held her breath and pulled David's hands away from his face. His left eyeball was radically misaligned. His pupil was displaced to the corner of the eye socket and blood covered his entire eye. During play, the little girl with the taffy in her mouth ran into David and the taffy stick had poked him in the eye. With a herculean effort, Eleanor forced back her emotions, so as not to upset her son. "Everything will be fine," she kept telling David. Frank would be home soon, and everything would be okay.

She put a pillow under his head and gently blotted the blood from his eye and face. She wrapped his face in moist towels. Instinctively she grabbed the St. John Neumann relic off the living room hutch and put it under David's pillow. Eleanor held her son in her arms and rocked him back and forth to soothe both him and herself. She didn't know what else to do. But where was Frank?

She could wait no longer for her husband. Action had to be taken. Eleanor gathered up her son and flew out to the car. On the way she told her other boys to tell their father she was going to the hospital. Fighting her way through rush hour traffic with her injured son lying on the car seat next to her took ten years off her life.

When they got to Frankford Hospital, the emergency room staff refused to treat David, claiming that they had no competence with eye injuries and they might do more damage than good. They recommended Wills Eye Hospital.

Eleanor was totally exasperated. Back she went into the late afternoon Philadelphia traffic. Only nervous energy and a mother's love sustained her now.

David was received at Wills Eye emergency room and he was there for the rest of the night. The doctors at Wills Eye Hospital are plentiful, and the best in the world when it comes to treating the eye. They told Eleanor that David would require a year of treatment, including medicine, therapy, eye exercises, and eye glasses. David would have to wear glasses for the rest of his life.

For the next three months David and Eleanor followed the doctors' instructions. Eleanor also took her son to the St. John Neumann shrine. Pointing to the body of the saint during one visit, Eleanor whispered to her son, "Ask this priest to help you." David asked for help.

At the three month mark, Eleanor took David to Wills Eye Hospital for his regular check-up. His doctor examined him and seemed perplexed. He called two associate physicians who were familiar with David's case and asked them to examine David. They conferred for an unusually long time and Eleanor began to become disturbed.

They then turned their attention to Eleanor and said to her quite plainly, "Mrs. Scholz, David's eye and vision are perfect. There is no sign of damage whatsoever. And there is no need for David to wear glasses or ever come back here again. We can't explain it. It's a miracle." Those were the doctors' exact words.

As Eleanor and David left the office, hugging each other with joy, the doctors continued to discuss the case among themselves, remaining totally confounded.

Eleanor and David for their part knew exactly what had happened. Their prayers to St. John Neumann had been answered. ∎

TRANSMITTING WAVES OF MIRACLES

Edward Glynn was like any other ten-year-old boy — active in sports, short in his attention span, and a little on the sloppy side. He was also an above-average student at Saint Mary's Elementary School which was near his hometown of Hampton, Virginia. Ed was typical in every way until he reached the fifth grade.

Early in his fifth grade year he began to experience persistent, severe, unexplainable pains in his stomach. He was sent to Hampton General Hospital in Hampton, Virginia where a battery of difficult tests (G.I. series, rectal exams) were prescribed for the little ten-year-old. Dr. Young Sung Hong, a gastroenterologist and liver specialist of fine reputation, in consultation with a team of other experts, diagnosed Ed's problem as Crohn's disease.

Crohn's disease is a chronic inflammatory bowel disorder that causes scarring and thickening of the intestinal walls. It often leads to obstruction of the intestines. In Ed's case, his condition would grow progressively worse, causing a gradual reduction in the absorption of vitamins, minerals and nutrients into his system. Scarred areas would have to be surgically removed throughout his life. He could look forward to frequent seizures of pain, and the loss of bits and pieces of his intestines through surgery over the years. By his late 20's or 30's he would have to be fed intravenously.

From the fifth to the eighth grade Ed attempted, as much as the disease would permit, to live a normal life. But intermittent cycles of excruciating abdominal pain, lasting for months at a stretch, proved almost incapacitating. Ed was treated with a powerful steroid called Prednisone when the pain became unbearable. His food intake would virtually come to a halt during these phases of pain. Ed would survive on a few saltine crackers and a few sips of milkshake each day for weeks, even months at a time.

In addition to limited food intake, Ed would be forced to lie down ninety-five percent of the time, due to the intensity of the pain and his general lack of energy. Ed's parents converted the living room couch into a make-shift hospital bed for him so he would still feel he was part of the family.

During these tough months, Ed would lie on the couch in his pajamas gray-complexioned and with dark circles under his eyes. Often he was doubled over with abdominal pain. His biological clock thrown off from lying down twenty-four hours a day, Ed began to stay up all night and sleep all day. His parents and brother and sisters comforted him as much as possible. Some mornings Ed's father would come into the living room before work, sit down on the couch and put his son's head on his lap.

Ed's one consolation at the time was a little Sony radio which he kept on the end table by his head. Late at night, when he couldn't sleep, he would listen to talk show host Larry Glick, whose program was broadcast from Boston. At night it came in clearly all the way down to Hampton, Virginia. Ed would even call up the station and talk to Mr. Glick and periodically keep him informed of his health status.

Ed missed so much school that the public school system sent him a private tutor. Amazingly, whenever Ed was healthy enough to attend school, even after a three month absence, he never had any trouble maintaining his above-average score.

The Glynns were practicing Catholics and, as could be expected, turned to their Church during these trying years. Their parish of Saint Joseph's in Hampton was operated by Redemptorist priests. Father John Weingert, C.SS.R., one of the parish priests, took a special interest in Ed. He supported the family and made frequent visits. The Glynns derived great strength from his friendship and considered him a member of the family.

In early 1983, Mrs. Glynn heard of a highly regarded specialist by the name of Dr. James Thorton who practiced at the Lankenau Medical Center in Philadelphia. She made an appointment with him for April.

Fr. Weingert offered to make the trip with the Glynns. He thought he could be of some assistance to them since he knew the city of Philadelphia quite well. In early April 1983 Ed, Mr. and Mrs. Glynn and Fr. Weingert set out for Philadelphia. It was going to be a very arduous journey for Ed. In intense pain, he could barely walk the few paces from his couch to the car. After driving north for a few hours, the foursome stopped at a roadside restaurant for lunch. Ed forced himself to go in the restaurant, but before the meal was served, he made his way back to the car by himself, overcome with pain and exhaustion.

After a few more hours of driving, they reached their hotel in Philadelphia. Fr. Weingert had arranged to stay with friends. Mr. and Mrs.

Glynn went out for dinner while Ed flopped onto the bed in their hotel room. His parents brought him some dinner, but he wasn't able to eat.

The next morning the Glynns picked up Fr. Weingert and then proceeded to the St. John Neumann shrine. Fr. Weingert had arranged to say Mass at St. John Neumann's tomb. This was not unusual since Fr. Weingert was a Redemptorist priest. All Redemptorists have a strong affinity with St. John Neumann. He had hoped that Ed, an altar boy, would serve the Mass, but all he was able to do was prop himself up in a chair in the sanctuary and watch his dad serve in his place.

After Mass Fr. Weingert blessed Ed with the first class relic of St. John Neumann, which was displayed in a wooden cross near the sanctuary for use by the faithful. Ed kissed the relic.

Then Fr. Weingert took the Glynns on a quick tour of the city. The Glynns dropped him off at a bus stop and went to a luncheonette. Their appointment with Dr. Thorton was scheduled for early afternoon.

As the Glynns approached the luncheonette, Ed said that he thought he might be able to eat something. But what really astounded Mr. and Mrs. Glynn was the fact that Ed was walking normally — erect, not enfeebled and bent over as he was only hours before at church.

Ed ate a full lunch and some of his father's plate, too. He claimed to be feeling quite well.

It was time for the appointment with the celebrated specialist Dr. Thorton. Dr. Thorton had studied Ed's medical records and was fully aware of Dr. Hong's tests which verified the severe scarring of Ed's intestines, and the diagnosis of Crohn's disease.

Dr. Thorton administered a rectal exam to Ed. After the exam Dr. Thorton explained to the family that there was no sign of scarring in Ed's intestines. He said that it was impossible for Ed to have Crohn's disease because in such a case the scars remain in the intestines for life. Dr. Thorton did not know what to think of the previous diagnosis made at Hampton General Hospital, nor of the x-rays indicating scar tissue, nor of Ed's three year battle with Crohn's disease. He brushed it off by proposing that perhaps it was just an isolated reaction of the colon. But he knew for sure that it was nothing serious like Crohn's disease.

The entire exam, consultation and rendering of the clean bill of health took less than an hour. No follow-up treatment or doctor's care was deemed necessary by Dr. Thorton.

That night, their last in Philadelphia, Ed wanted to go to a mall and play video games and buy a new pair of pants. At some point, as the Glynns joyfully strolled through the mall, it struck them: God had intervened. They were sure of it. As they assembled the events in chronological order, they saw no other explanation. They went out for an Italian dinner and Ed ate like any growing boy in his early teens.

Fr. Weingert called the Glynns at their hotel room that night to see how the examination went. They told him all that had transpired. Fr. Weingert was cautiously non-committal as to the supernatural character of Ed's recovery.

The next day the foursome arrived back at Hampton, Virginia. When Ed's brother and sisters went out to the car to greet them, they were shocked to see Ed walking erect with a spring in his step. He was energetic and smiling (something he had all but forgotten how to do). Especially pronounced was Ed's voice; it was deeper, stronger, more robust. The family rejoiced as they heard the account of the miracle. "But who was St. John Neumann?" they asked. The Glynns, though practicing Catholics, had never heard of him before. The former Bishop's story was then related to them.

One of the first things Ed did after his recovery was call Larry Glick to tell him of his miracle. Glick's broadcast transmitted the story of Ed's healing up and down the East coast. Many listeners heard the story of St. John Neumann's love for young people that night.

It is nine years now since the examination at Dr. Thorton's office and no sign or symptom of intestinal problems have reoccurred, nor has Ed been near a doctor's office.

POSTSCRIPT: Shortly after his recovery Ed entered the Redemptorist seminary. He is now 22 years old and studying happily at the Redemptorist novitiate in Esopus, New York. Ed hopes to be ordained a priest for the order in a few years, although (like any other seminarian), he is discerning and testing the spirits to see if this is truly God's will for him.

Ed believes that the seed of his vocation resided in his heart long before his ordeal and healing. He does not like to see his vocation and the miracle linked too closely together. It is difficult to say whether his desire to become a priest is directly associated with the favor granted through the intercession of St. John Neumann. Only God knows for sure. The Redemptorist order was the obvious choice since his primary contact with priests was at his home parish, run by the Redemptorists. Fr. Weingert fully concurs with Ed in these views regarding the miracle and his vocation. ■

Seminarian Edward Glynn of Hampton, Virginia was cured of a painful and debilitating case of Crohn's disease in 1983. He is pictured above with his niece Sheila.

BRIAN'S STORY

Brian Baker was the kind of child every parent would want. He was intelligent, compassionate, very affectionate with his parents and had absolute trust in them. His behavior was well ordered and he was mature, responsible, and courageous beyond his years.

Brian was the third child of Susan and Fred Baker of Greensburg, Pennsylvania, a small city forty miles east of Pittsburgh. They were both very proud of him as they are of their two other children Michael and Erin.

In early July 1986, when Brian was three years old, he woke up one morning vomiting violently. Susan thought it was just a virus. The same thing happened the next morning, and the morning after that. Susan and Fred wasted no more time; they took Brian directly to the hospital for an examination.

On July 7, a brain scan was done at Children's Hospital in Pittsburgh. The scan confirmed the existence of two malignant brain tumors, one on the top of Brian's brain stem and one on his pituitary gland. Susan and Fred saw their world crumbling before them, and they felt helpless as to what to do.

Surgery was called for and the team at Pittsburgh Children's Hospital performed a sixteen hour operation. Ninety-five percent of the tumor on the brain stem was successfully removed. But the pituitary tumor was inoperable. This tumor and the remaining five percent of the brain stem tumor would have to be treated with chemo- and radiation therapy. The prognosis was not good.

About two days after surgery, little Brian began to have seizures. While in a deep sleep, he would snap into consciousness and spring into a fit of thrashing, shaking and screaming. His eyes would be wide open, but he would stare right through his mother and father who were always at his side. He could neither see nor hear them despite their loving efforts to calm him. These outbursts always left the Bakers emotionally and physically drained.

After two days of these seizures, which occurred every fifteen minutes around the clock, medication was administered. Brian slept for twenty-seven hours straight. The Bakers were later to find out that these seizures were triggered by cerebral strokes caused by blood clots.

When Brian left the hospital he couldn't walk. No physical therapy was prescribed for him by the hospital staff. In hindsight, Susan realized that the staff didn't prescribe any rehabilitative therapy, which is normal routine, because they thought it would be pointless — Brian had little time left.

Towards the end of August, Susan came across the story of Michael Flanagan, which was picked up by one of the Pittsburgh newspapers on the occasion of his death by a heart attack. Michael Flanagan was the recipient of the healing from osteosarcoma in 1963, that was accepted as the third miracle for St. John Neumann's cause for canonization, as was mentioned earlier in this chapter.

Although the Bakers were members of Holy Cross parish in Youngwood (a suburb of Greensburg) and practicing Catholics, they had never heard of St. John Neumann. They called the Neumann shrine the very next day after reading the article and made arrangements for a visit. In late August Susan, Fred and Brian made their pilgrimage of faith to Philadelphia. Fr. Tom Lukac, a parish priest of Holy Cross church and a friend of the family, encouraged the trip.

The Bakers met one of the priests at the shrine and explained their needs. They were received warmly by this Redemptorist Father who went to a locked closet and pulled a cloth from the shelf. The body of St. John Neumann was laid on this cloth when it was being dressed for the canonization ceremonies. Some of the body fluids seeped into it. The priest gently and modestly rubbed Brian's head and body with this cloth and invoked God's mercy through the intercession of St. John Neumann.

A month later, Children's Hospital in Pittsburgh discontinued all treatment and sent Brian home. The staff said that there was no longer any sign of either tumor. Brian was able to walk, talk, and ride a bike normally.

The next three years were warm and wonderful for the Baker family. They were so very grateful to St. John Neumann for his intercession.

But then, in August 1989 Brian became pale and tired. Doctors at Children's Hospital identified an abnormal cell in Brian's blood. He had the symptoms of leukemia, but the hematologists could not verify that it was leukemia. Some treatment had to be administered to arrest the spread of this cell, so Brian was treated with chemotherapy used in cases of leukemia. He slowly deteriorated until he died at age six on January 5, 1990.

The Bakers firmly believe that St. John Neumann obtained for them three additional years with Brian that they would otherwise not have had. As Susan puts it, "We needed those three years to prepare for Brian's departure.

We could not have handled it in 1986." Susan and Fred are certain that St. John Neumann is behind the inner peace they have in accepting Brian's death. They didn't need any therapy, as so many do who lose a young son or daughter.

POSTSCRIPT: Some months after Brian's death, the Baker family was gathered in the living room one evening. Erin entered the room with a book of saints she recently received from Holy Cross grammar school. As the sisters at school had recommended, she was asking her family members their birth dates and looking up the corresponding saints' feast days. Erin told everyone the patron saint of their birthdays. Then, with a quizzical twinkle in her eye, she asked her mother a disarming question as only innocent children can do: "Mommy, does it count if the saint's feast day is the day you die?"

"Why do you ask, Erin?" Susan responded. "Well, because St. John Neumann's feast day is January 5, 1860. Brian died on January 5, 1990, didn't he?" questioned Erin.

Susan and Fred were stunned. They had never associated the two dates in that manner. Their shock was quickly transformed into joy as the significance of it became apparent to them. God had given them a clear sign regarding the well-being and whereabouts of their son Brian. No wonder they had such inner peace regarding his death. ∎

III

CANCER:
HIS SPECIALTY

St. Peregrine Lozios (AD 1345) is the patron saint of cancer victims and has aided many who have found themselves plagued by this malady. But in heaven one saint does not compete with another. All glorify God and fulfill the Divine Plan in accord with His holy will.

And so it is that St. John Neumann also seems to have cancer as one of his secondary specialties as well. Perhaps it is because cancer is one of the most devastating diagnoses being delivered these days, that God permits the compassionate St. John Neumann to address this suffering with healing and relief on many occasions.

The reason for St. John Neumann's effectiveness in dealing with cancer is known only in heaven. But the results are evident here on earth. This chapter includes one detailed case personally verified by the author. The other ten brief samples of St. John Neumann's triumphs over this disease were taken from the St. John Neumann Shrine files. Some requested to remain anonymous. (These ten are the only accounts not received by the author first hand.)

"HONEY, IS THAT YOU?"

The hand of Divine Providence weaves a mysterious and intricate pattern which makes up the tapestry of our lives. The pattern is at once ordered and random, and certainly unpredictable, as it is being woven by the hand of God. And it is not without both suffering and joy. When it is completed, it seems to fit perfectly into the grand design of God's handiwork.

Margaret Ratajcak's life is no different. She grew up and lived all of her fifty-five years in Woodbridge, a New Jersey suburb about twenty-five miles south of New York City. She now lives there with her husband Tom, sixty-two, a policeman for thirty years. Their children Thomas Jr. and Cynthia are now adults.

Their parish church is St. James, and Margaret has been a faithful parishioner since she was a little girl. Growing up, Margaret thought that she would like to be a hairdresser and did this for some years. But after her children got older, she went back to college and earned her degree. She now works at South Amboy Memorial Hospital, in Amboy, New Jersey as a medical librarian, a job which she has held for some years.

About twelve years ago Margaret first visited the St. John Neumann shrine with her parents on a special pilgrimage organized by the local Knights of Columbus council. She felt an immediate bond with St. John Neumann and joined the Neumann Guild, which is affiliated with the shrine. In subsequent years she went back to the shrine on many occasions privately with her husband.

Margaret developed such an affinity with St. John Neumann that she distributed medals, booklets, holy cards and other materials of St. John Neumann to her relatives, friends, children, and anyone who was open. She told his story everywhere, even visiting grammar school religion classes in her locality. Her bond with the saint seemed so natural to her. During these years of promotion Margaret never imagined that shortly she would be calling upon the saint for more than patience in a traffic jam.

On Labor Day weekend in 1987 Margaret was shopping with her daughter and two granddaughters at the Midstate Mall in East Brunswick, New Jersey. The girls wanted pizza for lunch, so they stopped at a little pizza parlor in the mall. The pizza came, hot and cheesy, and everyone dug in. On her second bite, Margaret heard a loud crack, like the breaking of glass, and felt a sharp pain at the base of her ear that continued around to the back of her head. Margaret thought she had broken a tooth, so she went to the ladies room, but found that all her teeth were intact.

That night her jaw swelled. The next day at a family cookout, her son-in-law, a chiropractor, examined her jaw and recommended x-rays.

The Tuesday after Labor Day Margaret was back on the job at the library at South Amboy Memorial Hospital. During her break she went up to see a friend in radiology. He arranged to have an x-ray of her jaw done immediately. An hour later she was called up to radiology again. The radiologist sat down with Margaret and explained to her that he could see something lying in her left jaw bone. He advised her that he was going to call an oral surgeon in on her case right away.

An appointment was set up that day with Dr. Santoro. He did a panoramic scan and discovered that something was definitely "sitting on her jaw bone." Dr. Santoro suspected that it was a cyst. He attempted to drain it with an aspirator, but failed. It turned out to be a dense, solid mass.

Two biopsies were done in his office and the results were sent to Memorial-Sloan Kettering Cancer Center in New York City, as well as South Amboy Hospital. In the meantime Margaret felt good, except for some slight swelling in her jaw. South Amboy Hospital analyzed the biopsy and determined that it was a benign tumor. Dr. Santoro scheduled one-day surgery to remove the tumor the next Friday, and Margaret and Tom breathed a sigh of relief. It would be a painful setback, but at least it wasn't cancerous.

A day or two before the scheduled surgery at South Amboy Hospital, Dr. Santoro called Margaret. "Margaret," he said, "we have some bad news. Sloan Kettering has diagnosed the mass as osteogenetic sarcoma of the left mandible." (Malignant bone cancer of the lower left jaw.)

Margaret was called to Sloan Kettering within a few days and met her specialist, Dr. Spiro. In a highly professional and direct manner Dr. Spiro informed Margaret that her entire jaw bone would have to be removed. Margaret, an attractive woman, slowly raised her hand to her face and gasped, "Oh my God, I'm going to be a monster."

Dr. Spiro quickly responded, "Young lady, get your priorities straight. Do you want a slightly deformed face or do you want to die?"

Margaret paused and then questioned, "What are my chances, doctor?"

Dr. Spiro (a Jewish physician) answered in all candor, "It's up to God above." Margaret later discovered that there was a ten percent survival rate in cases like hers. In fact, her type of cancer is so aggressive that in all probability she would be dead in three months.

Dr. Spiro explained to Margaret an overview of the treatment. It involved intensive chemotherapy prior to surgery and equally intensive post-operative chemotherapy after surgery and recovery. He warned her to be prepared to spend virtually one whole year in the hospital.

As Providence would have it, the week before Margaret's admission to Sloan Kettering a Redemptorist priest came to St. James church and conducted a parish mission. Margaret attended every session and prayed intensely to St. John Neumann for the whole week.

On December 18, 1987, in a twelve and one-half hour surgical procedure, Dr. Spiro and Dr. Hidalgo removed Margaret's left jaw bone, made a bone graft from her entire left tibia (fourteen inches long), fashioned it into a replacement for her left jaw and fastened it in place with plates and pins. The operation required a tracheotomy.

A few hours after surgery, Tom went to the hospital to visit his wife. He walked into the room she had for the weeks prior to the operation and came upon a person whose whole face was bandaged. It was the size of a basketball. Tom thought to himself, "I must be in the wrong room. Look at that poor soul." Tom stepped into the hall and checked the room number. It was his wife's room all right.

Tom stepped back into the room and whispered, "Honey, is that you?" Margaret blinked. Tom asked compassionately, "How you doing?" Margaret blinked again.

Margaret's recovery in Sloan Kettering was long and arduous. She prayed her way through it. A first class relic of St. John Neumann was applied to her jaw, face and chest daily. Soon Margaret was able to get around the hospital. She would visit other cancer patients young and old, Christian and Jewish alike, and pray with them and tell them about St. John Neumann.

After her grueling recovery, Margaret went home in mid-April 1988. She was cancer free, and by then all her blood and vital counts were normal. But her ordeal was not yet over. She had to have additional surgery done on the inside of her mouth. Her lower teeth, gum and jaw line needed to be corrected so that they would be functional enough to permit her to chew and eat properly. It would be a long process.

In November 1989, sixty-four plates, pins and screws were removed (her neck had to be opened for this operation). In January 1990 Margaret had extensive cosmetic surgery. The following March she had three quarters of an inch cut away from her entire right jaw to even it off with the left. In June five rods were drilled into her left jaw in preparation for dental work. In

November 1990 she had the bridge work done. These days Margaret has a functional set of teeth. The cosmetic surgery has all but erased any signs of her jaw and facial operations, and she leads an active, healthy life.

Doctors continue to marvel at Margaret's case. Her type of cancer usually reappears in six months. Now, four years later, they can't believe how good she looks.

Today Margaret is an apostle of St. John Neumann. She feels a special vocation to bring him to cancer patients. Consequently she has joined the American Cancer Society in order to fulfill this mission. Margaret is convinced of St. John Neumann's concern for those who suffer from cancer. In her own words she says, "I would not be here if it were not for St. John Neumann. My doctors were great, but it was all directed from above. I want to say to everyone—keep praying. When I got sick, I put myself in the saint's hands. My last thoughts, each time I drifted off under the pre-operative anesthesia, were of St. John Neumann. I knew he wouldn't let me down."

Margaret Ratajcak credits St. John Newmann with her complete recovery from cancer of the jaw. She is shown above in 1988, after her recovery.

NORMA DE MARZIO

NORMA DeMARZIO, PHILADELPHIA — In June of 1987 Norma went to the hospital complaining of back pains. After x-rays she was informed that she had bone cancer. She collapsed into a severe depression and her life lost all significance to her.

After further investigation, the doctors told Norma that she had "galloping" cancer — it was spreading like brush fire. She became sick to her stomach at this report.

In desperation, Norma ran to the Neumann shrine and begged the saint to let her live. After that she visited the shrine as often as she could, even when she was in pain. To her surprise and delight, the pain would disappear after each prayer session at the shrine.

Today Norma is fully recovered. She has no more cancer and no more pain. It seems to her as though the cancer was just a bad dream, but of course it was very real, as was the pain.

She loves St. John Neumann, and will be his devotee forever. She says, "If I had a million dollars, I would give it all to the shrine." ■

SUSAN STARTZEL

SUSAN STARTZEL, PHILADELPHIA — In December of 1984 Susan Startzel of Philadelphia was informed that she had inoperable cancer. The next five months were the most difficult of her life. She went to the hospital for cobalt and chemotherapy treatments with all of the negative side effects. The fight was a tough one and she got her strength to go on from her loving husband and five supportive sons, and her family and friends.

On Saturday, March 30, 1985 Susan and her husband made a visit to the Neumann shrine at Fifth and Girard. Susan was given the unique privilege of holding St. John Neumann's chalice. She kissed it and asked him to intercede.

On Monday, April 1, she went to the hospital for chemotherapy. Some tests were also taken to examine the spread of the cancer. The results were astonishing. There was no cancer in her body. She was cured of this painful and frightening disease. ∎

EDWARD DOMBROSKI

EDWARD DOMBROSKI, PHILADELPHIA—Edward never prayed to St. John Neumann in his life until he was sixty-seven years old. A couple of weeks before Christmas 1989 a biopsy revealed a malignant tumor in his chest. He was filled with overwhelming anxiety and apprehension.

One of the nuns in his parish (Holy Spirit) suggested that he pray a nine day novena to St. John Neumann. He also visited the shrine a number of times and attended the Mass when then-Archbishop Bevilacqua re-dedicated the refurbished shrine. From that time he has prayed to St. John Neumann daily.

Early in 1991 a bone scan, liver scan and spleen scan all proved negative, as did the lung x-ray. On January 12, he underwent an operation to remove the lump in his chest.

Since then he has had no pain, and after examination, his lymph nodes proved to be completely clear. No chemotherapy or radiation was necessary.

Edward thanks St. John Neumann for his intercession. ∎

ESTELLE VERKOWITZ

ESTELLE VERKOWITZ, HOLLIS HILLS, NEW JERSEY — In January, 1987 Estelle was operated on for breast cancer and had a mastectomy. Placing her trust in God, she took a relic of St. John Neumann with her into the operating room. The tumor was very large, and during the operation she hemorrhaged a great deal. Because of the size of the tumor removed and the amount of blood she lost, Estelle was not expected to return to the recovery room that day.

But she had a remarkable recovery. After only a few hours she consumed a large supper of solid food. It was expected that she would only be able to tolerate liquids. In fact, much to the pleasant surprise of the doctors, a few hours later Estelle asked for and ate a sandwich.

Estelle felt absolutely wonderful, and feels the same today. All of the post-operative cancer tests proved negative, and on two different occasions she heard the doctors murmur "amazing" with regard to her case.

She gives all the credit to St. John Neumann. ■

GINNY DAVIS

GINNY DAVIS, SARASOTA, FLORIDA — Ginny, a native of Philadelphia, was diagnosed with breast cancer so advanced that it was inoperable. Chemotherapy was prescribed, but it was of no avail in shrinking the mass, despite months of treatment. Ginny became frightened and depressed.

On a trip to Philadelphia from Sarasota, when she was visiting relatives, Ginny stopped at the shrine with a friend. Although not a Catholic herself, she had been to the shrine many times before and had become quite attached to the "little bishop" from her home town who became a saint.

Upon her return to Florida, she went for her usual checkup, only to find that the tumor had shrunk. In fact, a mastectomy could now be done. After the operation, there was no trace of cancer in her body.

All during this time she wore a relic of St. John Neumann and prayed for his intercession. Now, over three years later, she remains cancer free and is doing quite well.

Ginny is eternally grateful to her beloved saint.   ■

MARCIAL GUERRERO

MARCIAL GUERRERO, QUEENS, NEW YORK — Marcial, fifty-seven, was diagnosed as having a malignant brain tumor. The CAT-Scan revealed a mass the size of an orange; surgery was impossible. The doctors suggested chemotherapy.

Hearing of their hardship, a friend gave the Guerreros a St. John Neumann novena prayer card. The Guerreros made good use of it. Shortly thereafter, another MRI and biopsy were performed. The tumor was reduced to the size of an olive.

Marcial is much improved and continues to improve day by day. The doctors and experts are amazed by the case. The family absolutely attributes the turn for the better to St. John Neumann. ∎

BALTIMORE MAN

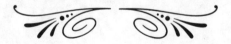

F.S., BALTIMORE — F.S. had surgery twice in 1978 for cancer of the colon. It was followed by chemotherapy. Six months later he had a serious relapse; while he was on his deathbed, a nun came to visit him. She had a relic of John Neumann and told F.S. to pray to him. He did so and five days later he began to recover. He has been on the mend ever since. At his last examination the doctors said, "Don't come back. You're completely cured of cancer." F.S. is convinced that St. John Neumann won the day for him. ∎

WILLISBURG MAN

MAN, EIGHTEEN – WILLISBURG, NEW YORK – A young man, age eighteen, was baptized, confirmed, anointed and enrolled in the Brown Scapular of Our Lady. The next day he made his First Holy Communion. The man was preparing for death. That same night he started a novena to Mary and Saint John Neumann. His prayer was that if he was not cured of the terminal cancer he had, God would give him the grace to suffer willingly and accept his fate.

The next morning the pain was completely gone; he ate and drank for the first time in a month without becoming sick, and the lump on his hip had disappeared. Ever since then he has been riding his bike, jogging and leading an active, happy life. No signs of cancer can be traced in his body. The doctors don't know what to make of it. ∎

THROAT CANCER

ANONYMOUS PILGRIM – In November 1972 he had a malignant goiter removed. He lost his voice almost completely due to this procedure. A friend enrolled him in the St. John Neumann Guild and he began to pray to the saint. He was scheduled for additional surgery, and he prayed earnestly to the saint the evening before his operation. When he awoke he was able to speak. The recovery was total, even though two specialists told him before the operation that he would never speak again. He continues to offer St. John Neumann a "full-throated" prayer of thanksgiving. ∎

YOUNG MAN

YOUNG MAN WITH CANCER – A young man, who desires to remain anonymous, lost his leg to cancer. This was a crushing blow to him because he was a great athlete. Soon the cancer spread to his lungs. He was sent a relic of St. John Neumann when he was at his lowest point.

Shortly after receiving the relic, the physicians informed him that no further treatment would be administered to him – he was totally cured.

The doctors were able to fit him with a prosthesis. He went on not only to play sports, but he even traveled to Europe with his college teammates to compete in a tournament with them.

He never ceases to thank St. John Neumann. ∎

IV

ASSORTED FAVORS

The next set of stories involves some unusual circumstances. They vary widely, but they all highlight St. John Neumann's concern for those in grave and desperate predicaments. Even skeptics will find these accounts arresting, especially the "Robbery on the Orient Express."

ROBBERY ON THE ORIENT EXPRESS

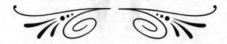

Mary Sukany was born and raised in the Kensington area of Philadelphia called Fishtown, between Third and Fourth Streets off Girard Avenue. She lived about two blocks from St. Peter's church, where her family attended Mass. Although the body of Bishop Neumann lies in state there now, when he was alive and well, some one-hundred forty years ago, he was known to have walked all over the territory of St. Peter's parish. Surely he had to have walked up Mary Sukany's street on many occasions, since it is only two blocks from the rectory. The Sukanys found it heartwarming to think that a saint had once roamed their streets.

The Sukany family can also claim another affinity with St. John Neumann. They are of Czechoslovakian descent and have the same ethnic roots as the saint who once strolled in their neighborhood. So when Mary was growing up, devotion to John Neumann seemed as natural to her as speaking Czech around the house with her parents and foreign-born relatives. It was just part of the tapestry of her life.

Mary attended St. Agnes grammar school and William Penn High School in the early 1940's. She was part of a little gang of girls who were as equally devoted to John Neumann as she was. Together this "gang" would walk up and down Girard Avenue to go shopping or to the movies. Invariably they would stop to visit St. Peter's and offer a prayer before the body of Bishop Neumann when they passed the church. Mary and her friends would never think of missing the Wednesday night novena to Our Lady of Perpetual Help at St. Peter's either. Such were the early years of Mary Sukany.

When Mary graduated from high school, she landed a job downtown, at Eleventh and Chestnut Streets, with fur merchandisers Mawson, DeMany and Forbes Furriers. She started in the accounting department and learned the business fast, working her way up to a high level management position.

She was also involved in lots of extra-curricular activities and organizations, including playing the organ at church. But the call was always there, like some distant echo that gently reverberated in her heart, especially during moments of quiet. It was for certain an interior conflict that would not leave her alone: how could she give up such a full and active life and become a nun? The change just seemed too radical.

In 1951, at twenty-four years of age, and after a vacation in Europe, Mary finally consented to the will of God. She entered the convent of the Sisters of Saints Cyril and Methodius, the nuns who taught her at St. Agnes Grammar School. Mary felt tremendous inner peace and joy in her decision. The move could truly be called a homecoming for her. Mary Sukany became Sr. Milada and began working to build up the Kingdom of God.

She was assigned to Danville, Pennsylvania and Charleston, South Carolina. Then she was sent to study at various Universities, including St. Joseph's in Emmitsburg, Georgetown, Seton Hall and Notre Dame. Sr. Milada, as she is commonly known, completed degrees in Education and attained a Masters in Business Administration.

Then she returned to Danville for a time and was even permitted to work in the Bronx with Mother Teresa and with immigrants in Appalachia. Finally Sr. Milada was sent to her present assignment at St. Cyril's Home for Retired Persons in Highland Park, Chicago. It should be noted that not only was Sr. Milada a fine educator and administrator, but was also a gym teacher and an accomplished gymnast, specializing in the rings and ropes. Her young students were always impressed by her strength and agility in gym class.

In 1977 Sr. Milada had the great privilege of being in Rome for St. John Neumann's canonization. She had been following the progress of his cause for sainthood over the years, and there was no way she would miss this great event. A triduum of devotions in honor of the new saint was held at St. John the Evangelist Church in Rome. A cardinal from the curia presided, many dignitaries and church officials were present and many hundreds of the faithful were in attendance also. Sr. Milada had been selected to do a reading in Czechoslovakian at one of the triduum services. She felt greatly honored to have had such a role in a service for the saint of her hometown, to whom she was long devoted. Sr. Milada would always remember those glorious days in Rome.

In 1981, between assignments, and after a number of years without a vacation, Sr. Milada was given permission to make another trip to Europe. She, her sister Agnes and her two cousins Martha and Mary comprised their traveling party. They planned first to try to enter Czechoslovakia, the country of their ancestors and the home of St. John Neumann. Then they intended to work their way west through Europe and take in as many points of interest as possible.

Czechoslovakia was still rigidly communist at the time, and they had some difficulty at the boarder getting entrance visas. Eventually they gained entrance and made their way to Prachatitz, the birth place of John Neumann. They gave the townspeople a relic and holy cards of St. John Neumann. These types of religious articles were not available to the Czech people under communist rule, and the villagers were very appreciative.

After completing their visit to Czechoslovakia, the foursome traveled westward by car for some distance, and then by train. Their planned itinerary included stops in Austria, Switzerland, France and Spain. At a certain point it was time for Agnes and Martha to return home. Sr. Milada and her cousin Mary continued westward by train through the beautiful countryside of Europe. They stopped at all the big cities. For Sr. Milada, who always loved Europe, it was a dream vacation.

Sr. Milada and Mary practically had the train to themselves. It was mid-autumn, an off-season for European travelers. So few passengers were traveling at that time of year that it seemed they had a whole train car to themselves.

On November 4, 1981 at about 10:30 PM Sr. Milada and Mary were waiting for their next departure at the train depot in Geneva, Switzerland. There they met Lucy, a Peruvian woman in her mid-forties. She was traveling alone. Realizing how uneasy one can feel traveling all alone in a foreign country, especially at that time of year, Sr. Milada invited Lucy to join her and her cousin. At first she declined. Then, discovering that Sr. Milada and Mary were going to Monaco and then on to Barcelona, just as she was, Lucy accepted the invitation. Seeing Sr. Milada in her full religious habit also helped to dispel Lucy's apprehensions.

The three ladies boarded the train for the 10:45 PM departure and selected a vacant compartment. Actually they had their pick. Almost every compartment was empty due to the sparse number of passengers that night. They conversed for a while, and then, around midnight, Sr. Milada said, "If we don't get some sleep, we'll be good for nothing in the morning when we get to Monaco. Good night, ladies."

Sr. Milada picked up her trusty little traveling bag, a kind of knit purse as it were, which contained all her valuables (cash, travelers checks, jewelry, fine rosaries and a relic of St. John Neumann). She worked her way down the dimly lit hall to a nearby empty compartment and stretched out across the seat, fully clothed in her habit. With her head by the window, she put her bag under her pillow for safe keeping and dozed off to the rhythmic sound of the train wheels clicking against the joints in the tracks.

At about 4:00 AM Sr. Milada roused herself from sleep for no apparent reason. Still dazed, she felt under her pillow only to find that her bag of valuables was missing. Striving to gain complete consciousness, she stumbled down the dim corridor, holding the hand rail to keep her balance as the train gently rocked back and forth. When she reached Mary's and Lucy's compartment she slid open the door. "Mary, someone stole my valuables!" she reported.

Sr. Milada was very distressed at the loss of her possessions and was ready to pull the emergency cord to stop the train, but she realized that the thief might slip off if she did. Down the poorly lit hallway, at the end of the train, she spied a lavatory. She was seized by a gripping hunch that the thief might be in there. A flow of adrenaline and righteous anger began to flush through her body, bringing all of Sr. Milada's faculties and senses into sharp focus. She called to her cousin Mary, and ran down the hall to the lavatory. She turned the handle. It was locked. Sr. Milada pounded her fist long and hard on the lavatory door.

Her determined persistence must have been intimidating. Within a few moments the door opened from the inside. Sr. Milada spontaneously took a quick, deep breath as she found herself face to face, with a fierce-looking twenty-six-year-old Arab man. As she looked into his eyes she could see them glistening with a mixture of indignation and fear. Glancing over his shoulder, she saw her bag on the lavatory sink. It was open.

Impulsively she reached past the man and grabbed the bag with her left hand. Sr. Milada deduced instantly that the thief might already have taken the contents and have them on his person. She instinctively clutched the thief's collar with her right hand so he couldn't escape. Sr. Milada's swift actions took him by surprise at first. Then he attempted to escape.

Sr. Milada felt herself losing her grip on his collar, so she threw a full headlock on him with her right arm. In this position Sr. Milada held the advantage, but she now found herself cheek-to-cheek with the thief. He continued to try to hedge down the hallway, pulling the two of them in the direction of the outside door.

Approaching the door, the young man struggled to gain the upper hand. He threw his body weight toward Sister, repeatedly slamming the two of them against the outside door. Sr. Milada was literally locked in mortal combat, and she knew it.

All this time Mary was screeching at the top of her lungs, virtually paralyzed by panic and disbelief. The car was empty. They were speeding across the European countryside at 160 kph (100 mph), utterly helpless, totally at the mercy of fate.

As Sr. Milada and her adversary wrestled, she could see that he was fumbling for the door latch with his free hand. It was then immediately clear to her that only a sheet metal door stood between her and death. No one could survive a plunge out of a train moving at a velocity of 100 mph. Time seemed to stand still as the battle for position intensified.

The thief found the latch with his free hand and desperately yanked open the door. When the door flew open, a deafening, tornado-like noise caused by the whirl of the wind, wheels, tracks, engines and moving parts pierced the corridor of the train car. It drowned out all other sounds.

He lunged for the opening, pulling Sr. Milada with him. Tumbling down a few steps with her nemesis, Sister sensed that she was being sucked out of the train. She reflexively grasped the hand rail with her left hand. She squeezed her five fingers over her bag, which was still in her hand, and clasped the rail with a death grip. The thief continued to tumble, and was now completely out of the train.

With her assailant's neck still locked in her right arm, her left hand fastened to the hand rail, and 100 mph winds coursing over her face, Sr. Milada literally felt like she was being torn in two. Another moment, and her left hand would fail. She had no choice but to release her right arm. The thief disappeared instantly, swallowed up by the black of the night.

Sr. Milada threw her right hand onto the hand rail. Now she too was totally outside the train. Her body became like a cloth flag flying in the wind horizontally. Her torso and legs flapped vigorously back and forth against the side of the train. It was pitch-black out. One second she was looking up at the stars, the next second she was staring into the ominous blackness that hid the steel tracks beneath her. The thunder of the 100 mph winds and the churning wheels just below resounded in Sr. Milada's head like a merciless death toll. No help was in sight. The former gymnast was losing her grip. How much longer could she hold on?

Mary was on her knees at the doorway screaming words of encouragement to her cousin. She was not able to get close enough to help her, or she too would be sucked into the "black hole." Neither could she leave her cousin to get help for fear that Sister would slip into the darkness at any moment.

Sr. Milada knew it was over. She prayed and prepared herself for death. Just then a shrill whistle blew and the train suddenly came to a grinding halt. Lucy, the reluctant traveling companion from Peru, had pulled the emergency cord and stopped the train.

With her last ounce of strength Sr. Milada pulled herself into the train. Her right leg emerged from the darkness, covered with blood. At first she couldn't see her right foot. She thought she had lost it while being whipped about against the train. She continued to hike her legs all the way into the car. Then her right foot finally came into view. It was severed, chopped off at the ankle. The foot itself was dangling at the ankle by a bloody sliver of flesh. It was black and blue, bleeding, and three times its normal size.

Four train personnel arrived at the scene. They were not trained in emergency medical techniques, so all they could do was carry Sister aboard and make her as comfortable as possible in one of the compartments. Sr. Milada received no medical attention until the train reached the next town, which was Tariscan. When they pulled into the station, the trauma unit was waiting. Sr. Milada was gently laid on the stretcher. She mentally prepared herself for amputation.

At the hospital, the doctors noticed that the large toe of her right foot moved. There was a chance to save it. So Sr. Milada was rushed to Joseph Imbert Hospital in Arles, France. She was wheeled directly into the operating room and the surgical team commenced immediately. Sr. Milada was administered a spinal, so she was conscious for the entire operation, which began at 7:00 AM and ended at 11:00 AM. During her two week stay there, additional surgery was necessary.

Five days after that infamous night on the train, the French police visited Sr. Milada at Joseph Imbert Hospital. At first they thought her story was a hoax. But they investigated Sr. Milada's allegations and found the body of an Arab man, about twenty-six, along the train tracks some miles east of Tariscan. He had bled to death from injuries he incurred when he plummeted from the train car. The police officers recovered Sr. Milada's possessions, which were in the thief's pockets, including the rosaries, which he tore apart, and the relic of St. John Neumann.

The police were able to identify her assailant; he was Mohammed Dekkiche, a professional thief and murderer. He was a wanted man, and known to be hitting high-speed trains in Europe. Fortunately for her, Sr. Milada did not wake up when he lifted her bag from beneath her pillow, while she lay asleep in the train compartment.

At Sr. Milada's insistence, she was transported across the Atlantic Ocean to St. Agnes Hospital in Philadelphia. She wanted to be there because it was established by St. John Neumann and staffed by an order of Franciscan sisters he founded when he was bishop of Philadelphia. She was there for six weeks.

Dr. Stephen Bassacio, MD was her attending physician at St. Agnes Hospital. At the end of the six weeks, Dr. Bassacio, an ordinarily calm, non-emotional man, was beside himself with joy. He excitedly romped through the hospital showing Sr. Milada's x-rays to all his colleagues. He was thrilled and astounded by her remarkable recovery. Sr. Milada of course knew it was the result of the supernatural intervention of St. John Neumann.

Today her right foot functions wonderfully. She walks three to four miles per day with absolutely no pain. The shape of her foot, ankle and leg is virtually normal. The sensation and nerve responses are fine.

Sr. Milada also wears the relic of St. John Neumann she had in her traveling bag on the occasion of that tragic night, ten years ago. It is fixed in the cross she wears around her neck. All of the sisters in her order wear a similar four inch cross as a symbol of their consecration to Jesus, but Sr. Milada's is special. A Jewish dentist was so impressed with her story that he crafted a four inch sterling silver cross and affixed the relic to the cross, as a gift for Sr. Milada. When Sister puts the cross on in the morning, she knows that she is protected; experience has proven it to her.

Sr. Milada is now happily fulfilling the duties of her vocation back at the St. Cyril home for Retired People in Chicago. Whenever she has the opportunity, she makes a pilgrimage east to her old neighborhood in Philadelphia in order to stop at the Neumann shrine and thank her friend.

When asked about her assailant, Mohammed Dekkiche, she says, "Whenever I hear the name Mohammed—which nowadays is so often in the news—I pray for him."

Agatha Christie's *Murder on the Orient Express* is surely a suspenseful novel, but fiction always pales in the face of truth.   ■

Sr. Milada Sukany, sister of Saints Cyril and Methodius, believes that she never would have survived her "nightmare train ride" without St. John Neumann's protection. The above photograph of Sr. Milada was taken in 1992.

FAVOR FOR A
DAUGHTER OF ISRAEL

At the turn of the twentieth century, many Russian Jews immigrated to America seeking civil liberty and a better lot in life. Rena Sinakin's parents were among them; her grandparents came from a rural village in Russia not far from the setting for the play *Fiddler on the Roof*.

Her ancestors included members of both the Orthodox and Conservative Jewish congregations. When they arrived at Ellis Island they began a new life. Her grandparents eventually began to assume many of the customs of their new homeland. But they also clung fast to many of their old traditions too. Tevye, the lead character in *Fiddler on the Roof*, would have been proud of them.

Rena Sinakin's Hebrew roots run even deeper than that. The name Sinakin, according to family tradition, is a combination of two words: Sinai — the name of the mountain where Moses received the revelations of God's covenant with the chosen people, and Kin — as in kindred or family relatives. Whether Rena can trace her family heritage all the way back to the times of Moses is impossible to verify. But she certainly knows that she is a pure-blood Hebrew and happy to claim such distinguished religious, historical and ethnic roots.

Rena, now forty-one, lives in Fox Chase, Pennsylvania with her daughter. She has achieved notoriety as a professional artist. Rena specializes in drawing fine portraits of individuals, both ordinary and famous. These portraits are remarkable for their ability to reveal the inner soul of the subject. Actor Lou Gossett and Rabbi Meir Kahave have been among her subjects. Nelson Mandella also hopes to have Rena draw his portrait when he next visits the United States.

Rena has been blessed in many ways, but she also has had a vicissitude that has followed her most of her adult life. Rena has a sister, Lisa, who has suffered from chronic clinical disorders over the years. Lisa was prescribed medication on various occasions to stabilize her emotional condition, but she refused to take it. To complicate matters, Lisa was diagnosed as having breast cancer at Sacred Heart Hospital in Chester, Pennsylvania several years ago. The cancer spread to her brain and the treatment left her a mere shell of her former self.

Rena would keep a watchful eye on her sister during these trying years. But then Lisa deserted her apartment in Philadelphia unannounced, and Rena lost contact with her for a year and a half. Rena had heard rumors that she was living on the streets. She constantly worried about Lisa.

On Friday, March 9, 1990, Rena and her good friend Mary Wicuschek, a Philadelphia Catholic, were shopping at Spring Garden Avenue and Fairmount Avenue for art supplies. On the way home, they found themselves heading north of Fifth Street, not far from Girard Avenue. Mary, who has long been devoted to St. John Neumann, suggested that they stop to visit the shrine. Mary had often suggested this to Rena when they were in the vicinity of the Neumann shrine. But Rena always felt a little uncomfortable about it.

Mary: Rena, the St. John Neumann shrine is just a couple blocks away. Let's stop in for a minute.

Rena: What for?

Mary: Well, just to make a visit. (Mary was surprised this time that her proposal was not brushed aside, as on previous occasions.)

Rena: Okay. We have a few minutes to spare before I have to pick up my daughter at school! We'll go in, Mary, if you keep it short.

Rena was in a Catholic church only once before, twenty-five years ago, for a wedding. As they entered the shrine Mary whispered to Rena, "Miracles happen here." Rena was skeptical.

Rena admits that she was simply going along with Mary out of curiosity. As she wandered through the church, she appreciated the interior decor from a purely artistic point of view. There was no religious significance in it for her.

She turned around to see Mary kneeling quietly at the foot of the sanctuary in front of a rectangular crystal case about eight feet long, in the front of the chapel. Rena came up behind Mary and looked into the crystal case at what she thought was a statue. Unbeknownst to her it was actually the body of St. John Neumann encased in an airtight crystal casket, the top of which is now used as an altar for Holy Mass. With the critical eye of an artist she thought to herself, "I could do a better job than that." She was commenting on the mask with a likeness of St. John Neumann, which is placed over the face of his decayed body.

Then Mary spoke to her in a low tone.

Mary: That's him. Ask for a miracle.

Rena: I don't need one. I'm healthy and happy and so is my daughter.

Mary: You have nothing to ask for?

Rena: Well, maybe I could ask him where my sister is.

Rena began to move closer. She stepped over the restraining gate and into the sanctuary and knelt in front of the crystal casket and touched the glass. She observed closely the features of the mask over St. John Neumann's face as well as his bishop's vestments. She was intrigued. Then Mary broke her concentration.

Mary: Rena, you can't go up there.

Rena: Why not?

Mary: It's off-limits. No one is permitted beyond the gate you stepped over.

Rena then turned her attention toward the body of the saint and addressed Bishop Neumann in what she recalls as a rather incredulous tone, "Well, St. John Neumann, maybe you can tell me about my sister, Lisa. Is she alive and well? And, O yes, show me a sign right away."

Mary was a little taken aback by Rena's tone, but she said nothing, realizing that Rena was not aware of the particulars of Catholic prayer.

Rena got up, went out of the sanctuary and walked over to the little museum adjacent to the chapel that contains artifacts from the life of St. John Neumann. A newly conceived interest in the saint had sprung afresh within her. As she surveyed the artifacts and read the accompanying captions, she began to respect this man who dedicated his life to good works. Rena came to the step on which St. John Neumann had breathed his last breath. She felt a good inner feeling about him. Her eyes dropped to her watch. It was time to go. She went to find Mary.

Rena drove Mary home and went to pick up her daughter from school. She had to quickly get her daughter home, attend to some business and then set out for a birthday party with her daughter. She would be on the run for the rest of the day and into the evening. Rena finally got in that night at about 9:30 PM. The light on her telephone answering machine was blinking.

She pressed the play-back button on the machine and the voice on the tape identified himself as Sergeant Davolos of the Delaware State Police. Sgt. Davolos had found Lisa wandering along the highway in a tough area of New Castle, Delaware. Through a rather unusual turn of circumstances, he was able to get Rena's phone number. He informed Rena where Lisa was and that she was alright.

Rena immediately called the Delaware State Police and asked for Sgt. Davolos. He was off duty for the weekend and could not be reached until Monday. No one else was familiar with Lisa's case.

Rena laid down the phone. She was dumbfounded. She had gotten what she asked for at the Neumann shrine, and only that—the whereabouts and condition of her sister.

It was an anxious weekend for Rena. She counted the minutes in suspense until she made contact with Sgt. Davolos on Monday morning. As it turned out, Sgt. Davolos was one of those exceptional persons of compassion who had gone above and beyond the call of duty. He had gotten to know Lisa, and took an interest in her plight. He made arrangements to have her admitted to the Delaware State Hospital, so that she would no longer have to live unattended in the seedy hotel where she had taken up residence. Sgt. Davolos had also pressed hard to overcome all difficulties in tracking Rena down. Rena was very grateful. She made plans to get to the Delaware State Hospital to visit Lisa and confer with her doctors, as soon as her schedule would allow.

Rena also wanted to express her thanks to St. John Neumann. On that same Monday she went back to the shrine. Finding one of the Redemptorist priests she announced triumphantly; "I have my sign—now I want my miracle! St. John Neumann, please make Lisa well!" Then she told the whole story to the priest.

In time Lisa stabilized and was released from the Delaware State Hospital to a special supervised home, for those not quite able to function in society on their own. Now Lisa has her own apartment, although she still requires some supervision. She is receiving job training, looks and feels much better, and is restored to a loving relationship with her family again. As for her cancer, she was given a two percent chance of living more than one year. She is now going on her fourth year and the cancer is still in remission.

Rena is convinced that "this is miraculous." She has been strengthened in her own faith in God and in her belief in the power of prayer. She says that, "in the Divine Plan God must have known that I needed my prayer answered." The Orthodox Jewish believers in her family all love to hear Rena tell of her miracle.

From time to time Rena will visit the shrine. As for asking for any more favors, she puts it this way, "If I ever need something big, I will go to St. John Neumann. But I won't preoccupy him with trivial matters. Others need him for more serious things."*

---

* The portrait of St. John Neumann on the cover of this book was drawn by Rena Sinakin.

GANG FIGHT IN
MAPLE SHADE

In the summer of 1971, the Jay-Cee carnival in Maple Shade was the place to be. Held annually on the grounds of the Steinhauer school, the carnival featured rides, food, games, music and a beer hall. All the usual fanfare of lights, crowds, noise and the gala atmosphere that accompanies such events was evident. If you were a Maple Shade teenager you would "be there or be square."

Catherine Kain's son Bill had been going to the carnival for several years now. He went every night. Catherine's last words to her son that night as he left with his friends were, "Be careful, Bill." He threw a quick "Yeah, Mom," over his shoulder as he walked out the door, a little embarrassed that his mother still talked to him that way. After all he was eighteen now, old enough to drink in the state of New Jersey at the time. The beer gardens at the carnival were fair game for him. He and his friends had, of course, every intention of beginning their night at "the gardens."

Catherine settled down for an evening of worrying and tense anticipation that is so common to the mothers of all teenagers and young adults who go "out on the town." One parent likened his wait for his teenage sons and daughters return home after a party to that of an air force commander at the front: "I feel like a commander back at the air base waiting for the return of his pilots who flew out into dangerous enemy air space: I gaze up into the sky, wondering if they will ever return from their mission."

Another Maple Shade resident and a friend of Catherine's, Mary Johnson, also went to the carnival. She had taken her Down's Syndrome daughter to the carnival for some fun and diversion. Suddenly a riot broke out near the beer gardens. Some ruffians who had been drinking beer were now beating another teenager senseless. Mary saw them surrounding a boy, who was lying on the ground, like a wolfpack. One of their gang, who went by the name of Suds, was brutally kicking the victim on the ground in the face. The others circled around and cheered him on. Mary feared for her daughter and quickly left the carnival.

Meanwhile Catherine Kain was trying unsuccessfully to relax at home. The ring of the telephone shattered the silence and caused her heart to pound.

On the line was the mother of one of Bill's friends: "Catherine, you better come over here right away—your son Bill is here and he's hurt pretty bad."

As Catherine arrived at the house, Bill was being lifted into the ambulance. He was taken directly to the emergency room of JFK Hospital in Cherry Hill. Bill had been kicked in the eye and seriously injured. Dr. Brezaliere informed Catherine that something behind Bill's right eye was cracked, and he was hemorrhaging badly.

For ten days after the emergency surgery Bill was not permitted to move his head. It was touch and go. If the blood rose above a certain level, he would be blinded.

A very dear friend of Catherine's gave her a first class relic of St. John Neumann. Her only connection to John Neumann until that time was the one year she spent at the St. Peter's Annex to Hallahan High School on Fifth and Girard in 1938. Catherine put the relic around her son's neck and prayed with all her heart.

Bill recovered. Catherine and her husband thanked Bill's attending physician (a Jewish man), for what he had done and he replied, "Don't thank me, thank the Man upstairs." During one of Bill's later eye examinations his Jewish doctor said to one of his associates, "Take a look at this." The background of Bill's case was explained and the other doctor was amazed. The Jewish physician again stated, "That's a miracle."

Catherine credits St. John Neumann for her son's recovery, and so does her husband, a Protestant. In subsequent years, Bill, Catherine and the family have turned to St. John Neumann in all difficulties.

POSTSCRIPT: Later Bill developed an acute case of diabetes. By the time he was twenty-five years old he had to take daily injections of insulin. Despite this he was able to live a normal life. At thirty-eight, complications developed from the diabetes and he fell into a coma and remained that way for a few days, slipping in and out of consciousness. He implored his mother, "Mom, don't ask me to hang on, I'm ready to go."

Bill looked so tired and worn that his mother changed her mind about asking for a miracle. She asked St. John Neumann just to take care of him and not let him suffer. Bill, not worried, made his good-byes to his loved ones, and shortly thereafter departed peacefully. In a letter to Catherine his physician wrote, "Bill was a fine gentleman and highly respected and well thought of by the hospital staff. We will never forget your son."

SAVED FOR A PURPOSE

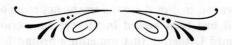

The Leaders are a close-knit family from Pennsauken, New Jersey who have always supported and rallied around one another. In early October 1986 they were to be truly put to the test. At that time Geraldine (known as Gerry) was forty-four, her husband Bob, a systems programmer, was forty-seven, and their two daughters Gerrianne and Lisa were twenty-four and twenty-one respectively.

Lisa, a nursing student in 1986, came home from school on Thursday, October 2 and found her mom in the kitchen.

Lisa: Mom, there's a problem with the car.

Gerry: What's the problem, Lisa?

Lisa: It keeps pulling to the right, like it's going to turn over or something.

Gerry: Okay honey, your father and I will take a look at it.

Lisa went up to her room and Gerry logged the news into her memory with all of the other items she would discuss that night with Bob. The rest of the day passed rather uneventfully.

In late afternoon Gerry realized that her mother-in-law had her regular check-up at the doctors for her heart and blood pressure that day. Bob was not home from work yet, and Mrs. Leader didn't live very far away, so Gerry planned to take her to the doctor's office, as she always did. Gerry also figured that this would give her a chance to test-drive the car. She considered herself a safe driver and assumed that the risk would be minimal.

As she drove to her mother-in-law's house, she could see what Lisa was talking about. The car pulled to the right. Something was definitely wrong.

Gerry finished her mission of mercy and was on her way home after dropping off Mrs. Leader. It was about 7:45 PM. She was traveling east on Federal Street near Marlton Pike in Camden, New Jersey, about three miles from her home.

In the darkness Gerry never saw the pothole in the road. Upon impact the car jolted. With frightening suddenness, the steering system locked and the car spontaneously accelerated. It slammed into a wooden telephone pole, which snapped in two. The car engine came through the dash and smashed into Gerry's legs. She was thrown onto the floor of the passenger's side and pinned under the dash.

"The gas is leaking! . . . The car is going to explode! . . . We'll never get her out in time." In her last moments of semi-consciousness before she slipped into a coma Gerry heard these words. In her dreamlike state she thought that they were talking about someone else. But she was the one who was trapped. Fortunately the rescue team was able to free her from the wreck in time with the "jaws of life."

Gerry was rushed to the Cooper Medical Center Trauma Unit in the city of Camden. Her body was demolished — her jaw was smashed, her right eye socket was seriously damaged, her nose was crushed, she had swallowed half her teeth and the other half were still imbedded in the steering wheel, nearly every bone in her face was broken, her pelvis was fractured in four places, both her legs were broken along with her right ankle, her gall bladder was ruptured, her spleen was injured beyond repair, and a main artery from her heart was damaged. By the time Gerry arrived at the operating room her right leg was already black and it was fully expected that an amputation procedure would be necessary.

That night a team of six surgeons, two trauma specialists, two orthopedic specialists and two plastic surgeons spent thirteen hours in the operating room with Gerry. The next day Gerry was profoundly comatose. Her body was degenerating and her vital signs were falling. Her doctors gave her ninety-five-to-five odds — a five percent chance of survival. This was Gerry's condition for the next two days.

Bob, Gerrianne and Lisa were wasted with anxiety and fear. The daughters always had an especially close relationship with their mother. Bob was at the hospital all day, every day, keeping vigil in the critical care waiting room.

Word of Gerry's accident traveled fast through her parish of St. Peter's, in Merchantville, New Jersey. Flora Fingerhut, a fellow parishioner, friend and neighbor, heard the news when she returned home from a retreat on Sunday evening, October 5.

Flora and her son John went immediately to the Leader's home and spoke with Bob. They gave him a first class relic of St. John Neumann and instructed him to place this relic over Gerry as soon as possible. They also gave Bob a short biography, a second class relic and novena prayer cards of the saint. "Pray this novena with your two daughters, and you can count on our prayers," implored Flora.

Bob returned to Cooper Hospital that night. It should be noted that Bob is not one to be demonstrative in the expression of his faith. But his beloved wife's life hung in the balance. The doctors now told him that it was just a matter of time. Infection had set in and Gerry's condition was deteriorating.

Realizing that God was their only hope, Bob took the first class relic of St. John Neumann and made the sign of the cross over each part of Gerry's battered body, and pinned the second class relic to her gown. He begged God to save his wife, and so did Gerrianne and Lisa.

On Wednesday, October 8, Gerry came out of the coma. Color returned to her right leg. She began to see out of her right eye again. Gerry continued to make progress.

When Gerry first emerged from the coma she asked, "What happened?" She was told that she had been in a serious car accident. Gerry ran her tongue across her once beautiful set of teeth and felt only gums. She cried. But as the whole story was revealed to her she was thankful to be alive.

Gerry had no doubt that St. John Neumann was at work in her recovery. Had she been conscious, she would have employed the same regimen of novenas and blessing with the St. John Neumann relic as Flora had recommended. Gerry had a long-time devotion to the saint herself. In 1956, as a freshman, she attended the St. Peter's annex of Hallahan High School at Fifth and Girard in Philadelphia. There she learned about St. John Neumann and developed a strong personal friendship with him that would last her whole life. From then on, whenever she needed help she called upon the saint.

Since October 2, 1986 she and her family have had to call on him frequently. Despite her extraordinary recovery, Gerry underwent fifteen major operations in the weeks following her accident. She spent six weeks in the trauma unit and another four weeks on the orthopedic floor at Cooper Hospital. When she came home she spent most of her time in a hospital bed and the remainder in a wheelchair. The doctors told her that she would never walk again.

Over the next five years she made eight trips to hospitals (mostly Cooper) and had thirty-five major surgeries and grueling post-operative recoveries. Gerry has been in and out of rehabilitation and physical therapy ever since the accident. In July 1987 she fought and prayed her way to self-sufficiency, even walking short distances. In September 1987 she began working again as a school administration aide. Dr. Flanagan of Wills Eye Hospital who worked on Gerry's right eye can't understand how she can see out of it today.

But Gerry knows how she had made all of this phenomenal progress; it has been with the help of St. John Neumann and the support of her family and friends. But the pain and discomfort are ever present. Her orthopedic specialists feel that she will need more corrective surgery in the future. Each new operation, post-operative recovery and subsequent period of rehabilitation take a tremendous toll on Gerry both physically and psychologically.

The corrective surgeries are scheduled at lengthy intervals to give Gerry a chance to gear up physically and psychologically for the next one. Once a person's bone structure is so thrown out of kilter as were Gerry's, corrective surgery can be almost a perpetual necessity. God seems to be the only One who is able to properly assemble the human body so that all parts work together in harmony.

Gerry's spirit is indomitable. Between operations, provided the pain level is not too intense, she is cheerful, works, attends to the family needs and is full of life. She always offers up her pain and suffering for worthy intentions. She prays daily and finds relief from physical pain and spiritual solace in prayer, especially when it is directed to the Blessed Mother and St. John Neumann.

Today Gerry is a proud and active grandmother. Her daughter Gerrianne and her son-in-law Tim Cammarota had their first child, Nicole Marie. She is the new joy in Gerry's life.

Gerry firmly believes that with St. John Neumann's assistance she will some day walk long distances again and use her wheelchair only on rare occasions. Somehow this doesn't seem far-fetched. ■

HE WILL FINISH THE JOB

The first time Tommy Tenaglia jumped in the water he proved himself to be a natural. Competitive swimming came to him as naturally as eating and sleeping. A Marlton, New Jersey resident, he attended Cherokee High School and swam for both Cherokee High and the Wahoos Swim Club in Mt. Laurel, New Jersey and did well.

Tommy was also gifted with a fine intellect. He scored 1200 on his S.A.T.'s and was an honor student. His life was rounded out by his family and his attendance at Sunday Mass at St. Joan of Arc church in his hometown.

On September 25, 1990 Tommy was driving home in the family jeep from a Cherokee swim meet with two teammates. At seventeen he was on top of the world. He had plans to be an engineer. He was discussing with his friends which college offer he should accept, Lehigh or Penn State. Excited talk of colleges and careers filled the jeep that night. It was almost 11:00 PM and they had school the next day, but they were already on Willowhead Road in Marlton, not far from home. Besides, the boys were discussing important matters, and time seemed irrelevant.

It happened so fast that they bearly had time to brace themselves. Tommy lost control of the jeep and struck a telephone pole. The momentum of the jeep kept it in motion as it flipped over three times. Each time the jeep flipped, one boy was hurled out of the vehicle. On the third flip Tommy was flung out of the jeep and lay unconscious on the street.

The New Jersey State Police Medivac unit responded quickly. Amazingly, Tommy's two friends suffered only minor injuries. But Tommy had to be airlifted to the Cooper Medical Center Trauma Unit in Camden, New Jersey for emergency treatment.

When Tommy's mother Kathleen arrived at Cooper Hospital she was given a status report: Tommy was unstable; had serious head injuries; five broken vertebrae, two of which were crushed around his spinal column; and a broken arm. Tommy remained unstable for twelve days. He underwent fifteen hours of delicate spinal surgery over a fifteen day period. He was kept under close watch in the neuro-intensive care unit for a month. Tommy was comatose for three months, and during this period had a major bout with pneumonia.

The doctors were very concerned about the massive head injuries he received. They said that "every part of his brain was bruised, including his brain stem." The doctors explained that the prognosis was poor. If Tommy did not improve by Christmas, he would most probably be permanently paralyzed or severely brain-damaged. It was also possible that he might never come out of the coma.

While still comatose Tommy was transferred to the AI DuPont Institute in Wilmington, Delaware, which specializes in head injuries.

From the second day of the injury on, Kathleen Tenaglia and her family made frequent pilgrimages to the St. John Neumann shrine. The saint had already worked a wonder in Kathleen's family life and so she had great faith in the power of his intercession.

About fifteen years earlier, Kathleen's five-year-old daughter, also named Kathleen, suffered a ruptured aneurysm of the brain that caused the little girl to go into a coma for six weeks. At the urging of Kathleen's three aunts, who are Glen Riddle Franciscan sisters (an order of nuns established by John Neumann when he was Bishop of Philadelphia), Kathleen blessed her daughter continually with a first class relic of St. John Neumann given her by her aunts. Today young Kathleen is doing very well. She graduated from college and is working full time.

Turning again to the saint, Kathleen placed the same relic on her son Tommy every day and visited the shrine every Saturday with her husband Thomas Sr. and her daughter.

During the month of December, deemed critical by the doctors, Tommy began to recover. On Saturday, January 5, (the Feast of St. John Neumann) the family took Tommy to the shrine in a wheelchair for the 10:00 AM Mass. After Mass they assisted him in kneeling before the body of Bishop Neumann for a brief prayer. It was an emotional moment for the whole family.

The Tenaglias continued to visit the shrine and Tommy continued to recover. Today he is fifty percent improved and still improving, albeit slowly. He is speaking, playing basketball, tennis and other individual sports. (For his safety, the doctors do not want Tommy to play contact sports, to avoid the possibility of a second injury.) He lives at home, is happy, and goes daily to the AI DuPont Institute, working towards total rehabilitation.

The Tenaglias are absolutely convinced that through the intercession of St. John Neumann "they have their son back, and [they] are very grateful." The doctors at Cooper gave them little hope, and the family feels that his recovery is miraculous. They now keep pictures of their "family intercessor" all over the house and pray every night that St. John Neumann will finish the job he has so wonderfully begun. ■

V

THOSE WHO SAW HIM

These last two accounts are phenomenal. They have to do with sightings of St. John Neumann over 100 years after his death. Is it possible? Theologically, it is (See Appendix IV: Visions). Did it happen in these cases? Let the reader be the judge.

"WHO WAS THAT STRANGE PRIEST?"

Thomas Kelley was born on Christmas eve, 1923, at Seventeenth and Tioga Streets, in Philadelphia. He was delivered at home, not unusual for the day. As Tom grew up he lived in a number of places in Philadelphia, including Incarnation parish near Duncanon Street, Holy Child parish on Broad Street and St. Martin of Tours parish on Roosevelt Boulevard. He attended North East Catholic High School. There he encountered the priests of the Oblates of St. Francis de Sales who operated the high school.

Inspired by their manly and spiritual example, he joined the Eastern province of the Oblates of St. Francis de Sales upon graduation from high school. The order sent him to study philosophy and theology at Catholic University in Washington, D.C. He was ordained an Oblate priest in Wilmington, Delaware in 1953. Fr. Kelley's first assignment took him to Bishop Duffy High School in Niagara Falls where he taught, coached and directed the athletic program. In 1957 the Oblates gave him permission to join the United States Navy, and he became a chaplain. He spent twenty-eight happy years as a Navy chaplain until he retired in 1986. (Retirement is mandatory at sixty-two. He would rather have stayed in the service.)

During those twenty-eight years Fr. Kelley served two sea duties on naval vessels, and spent time at naval bases and naval hospitals in Florida and New York. He then transferred to the Marines where he was a chaplain at Parris Island, South Carolina and San Diego, California. Fr. Kelley also served three years in Vietnam. His final assignment in the service was at Okinawa. As a priest, Fr. Kelley found these years very fulfilling.

Between tours of duty in September of 1975 he was on leave to celebrate twenty-five years as a priest. During this break he found time to visit his relatives in Philadelphia. On September 29, Fr. Kelley was having dinner at his brother Martin's home in Philadelphia. It was a long time since he had seen his brother and they chatted for hours.

Towards the end of the evening Martin, an oral surgeon, remarked to his brother that he didn't look well. Fr. Kelley confided to his brother Martin that he had been experiencing some tiredness during his last tour of duty at Parris Island. Even after a good night's sleep the fatigue persisted. Fr. Kelley attributed this tiredness to long working hours and the high humidity on base at Parris Island. Martin prevailed on his brother to come to Holy Redeemer Hospital in Philadelphia for a check-up the next day. Since Martin was on the staff, he assured Fr. Kelley that there would be no delay.

The next day, September 30, Fr. Kelley arrived at Holy Redeemer Hospital. Blood was drawn, a chest x-ray was taken and a brief consultation was conducted. The blood analysis indicated a problem: Fr. Kelley had been bleeding internally. Fr. Kelley then admitted that he was experiencing an "uncomfortableness" in the appendix area, and the staff requested that he stay overnight for a lower GI series. Father complied.

Martin was tense about the whole situation because in April 1974 Fr. Kelley and he buried their mother and in September 1975 they buried their aunt. Both died of colon cancer.

On October 1, the GI series revealed a mass around Fr. Kelley's appendix area. Martin and three of his associates entered Fr. Kelley's room. Martin, with all his experience on the floor, couldn't disguise the worry on his face. After all, it was his brother.

They informed Fr. Kelley of their findings, and made it clear that the mass was probably colon cancer. His family medical history, age, symptoms, etc., all pointed to this conclusion. During their thirty minute briefing, Martin and the other physicians summarized effectively the seriousness of the case.

After this, nothing else could be said. Martin and the doctors filed out of the room in silence. Fr. Kelley was stunned by the announcement. He sat reflectively for a long moment on the edge of his bed as the full impact of his condition penetrated his consciousness.

As the initial jolt of the prognosis subsided, Fr. Kelley's reaction became one of silent resignation to the cancer and whatever repercussions it might have. Surprisingly, he was untroubled by fear, but at the same time sobered by his knowledge of the cancer. Having served as a chaplain at several hospitals, he saw firsthand how ruthless a disease it can be.

Jumping ahead to the next consideration, he pondered the pros and cons of surgery. He had seen many patients come into a hospital with a cancer diagnosis like himself not seeming too ill. After surgery they took a turn for the worse and stayed there for their remaining months, awaiting death. He thought that he would prefer not to have surgery.

"Didn't you hear what the doctors said, Father?" The voice shattered Fr. Kelley's concentration. It was his roommate, a thirty-five-year-old Jewish man suffering from colitis. He had overheard the doctors' briefing and he was mystified by Fr. Kelley's low-key reaction. "If that was me, I would have fainted!" Fr. Kelley could only shrug his shoulders. "What can I do about it?" he calmly replied.

Fr. Kelley gently returned to his inner thoughts, reviewing his life and contemplating his end. A man's soul-searching can be no more profound than when he knows that the hour glass is spent and he is almost out of time.

Then a priest walked into the room. Fr. Kelley had already come to know the hospital chaplain very well. But he did not recognize this strange priest who was now calmly walking around his roommate's bed in full view, and coming toward him.

This priest wore a black suit, white collar and traditional black clerical vest, the dress priests wear today on formal occasions. The priest was slightly built, short, slender and in his mid-forties. He seemed to Fr. Kelley to be a gentle man who was in no hurry.

Without introducing himself the priest addressed Fr. Kelley: "Father, I understand you have a tumor?" Then the priest pulled a small object from his pocket. "I have a relic of John Neumann." He then placed the relic to Fr. Kelley's lips and also to his appendix area. The priest blessed Fr. Kelley, and said nothing else. He departed in the same manner in which he came, never identifying himself.

Although the idea of a relic of John Neumann at first seemed unusual (he was Blessed at the time), the name of John Neumann was not new to Fr. Kelley. Having been educated in Catholic grammar and high schools in Philadelphia he could name all of the former Bishops of Philadelphia. In fact he remembered during his Philadelphia days that South East Catholic was renamed after Bishop Neumann.

On several occasions Fr. Kelley described the mysterious priest that he and his roommate had seen to the hospital chaplain, to his brother Martin and to the nurses. No one had a clue as to his identity. But Fr. Kelley, an experienced hospital chaplain himself, was aware that many parish priests visit patients at hospitals. He gave no more thought to the incident.

Fr. Kelley spent the remainder of the day thinking about his condition. His general health was good, he thought to himself. But what if the surgery revealed the worst case scenario? How long would he have?

Fr. Kelley thought it best to transfer to the Philadelphia Naval Hospital. He did so the next day with all his medical records. The Naval physicians felt that immediate surgery was required. They operated on October 6, and the initial post-operative prognosis was very bad. Fr. Kelley had a Dukes class-B tumor of the colon in an advanced stage. It had erupted through the intestinal wall and the cancer cells were undoubtedly spreading to his other organs.

Fr. Kelley was hospitalized for five months after the surgery. Despite the fact that the operation was successful, the doctors were sure that because his colon was perforated, the cancer was invading other parts of his body. The situation was tense. Fr. Kelley was subjected to bone scans, liver scans, bone marrow biopsies with syringes and all manner of tests and examinations. He was given 4,500 rads of radiation therapy as a precaution. Fr. Kelley was ill during these months, but he never experienced any pain. Having been such an active man and hard worker, the confinement was trying.

In late March 1976 Fr. Kelley was feeling well enough to take a limited duty assignment with the Navy in South Carolina. Eventually his health was completely restored and he resumed his normal activities.

In May of 1976 a lot of publicity about John Neumann's cause for canonization was appearing in the news media. Fr. Kelley still maintained a subscription to the Philadelphia Archdiocesan newspaper the *Catholic Standard and Times* to keep up on events in his home town. Of course the *Standard and Times* ran many stories and photographs of John Neumann because his canonization was imminent. When Fr. Kelley picked up the first of such copies and opened it, a picture of a priest leaped out at him and seized his undivided attention. He peered at the picture long and hard. "No! it couldn't be! . . . Why me? . . . How could I ever forget that day!" Images of the room at Holy Redeemer Hospital raced through his mind. Portraits of the mysterious priest flashed in his memory.

Although that newspaper photo and the mysterious priest who blessed him with the relic of St. John Neumann at the hospital were identical, Fr. Kelley simply relates the facts and events as they transpired. He makes no categorical judgments or interpretations. It should be noted that Fr. Kelley began carrying a relic of the saint, praying a novena in his honor daily and experiencing a strong affinity for Bishop Neumann since opening the newspaper that day.

What Fr. Kelley does know is that for the next fifteen years his ministry has been extraordinarily fruitful, and that he "called on St. John Neumann for everything." In his own words he says that, "I have great reverence for St. John Neumann and I am certain that he has had a singular influence in my life over the past fifteen years."

Since retiring from the Navy in 1986 he still works full time in Beaufort, South Carolina with the Oblates of St. Francis de Sales in parochial, hospital, nursing home and family ministries. His annual medical checkup is still reading excellent.

The above picture of Fr. Thomas Kelley, priest of the Oblates of St. Francis de Sales and retired Captain of the United States Navy Chaplain Corps, was taken in 1991. Fr. Kelley received a mysterious visit from a strange priest strongly resembling St. John Newmann while in the hospital preparing for cancer surgery in 1975.

MIRACLE ON
34TH STREET*

It was 1983, three weeks before Midnight Mass, and Nancy and Chuck McGivern were preparing for a marvelous holiday with their children. Their home is in the Lower Mayfair section of Northeast Philadelphia near Bustleton Avenue and Devereaux Street where Christmas is still celebrated with traditional gusto.

On Thursday of that third week before Christmas their seven-year-old boy named Chuck Jr. was sent home from school with an apparent case of chicken pox. On Friday he lost consciousness and Nancy knew he had something worse than the chicken pox.

He was admitted to Rolling Hill Hospital and soon after to Children's Hospital of Philadelphia. At Children's Hospital the problem was diagnosed: he had a rare disease of the nervous system, brain and liver called Reye's Syndrome—a disease that is almost unique and usually fatal to children.

The doctor's tried to keep Chuck comfortable, but they could do little to stop the advance of the disease. By the time Nancy and Chuck Sr. got to his room at Children's Hospital he was white and cold, his body hard. Nancy gasped at the sight of the many tubes that attached her son to various life-sustaining machines and monitoring devices. The worst was a large steel bolt inserted through Chuck's skull. It was there to relieve and gauge pressure on the brain. The physicians said that if the gauge registered seventeen points, Chuck would be a vegetable—if he survived. But this was not likely.

---

* Much of the material for this account was taken from Frank Rossi's story in the Philadelphia Inquirer, Dec. 21, 1989, of the same title.

Nancy and Chuck Sr. had no other recourse but prayer. Her cousin had given her a relic of St. John Neumann. When she was a child her aunt used to take her on the trolley down to the shrine at Fifth and Girard for novenas. But that seemed so long ago.

In desperation Nancy threaded three religious medals on a safety pin, placing the St. John Neumann medal in the middle, and pinned them to the pillow case next to Chuck's head. Nancy and Chuck Sr. prayed and hoped and waited.

Chuck's condition worsened. The bolt in his skull registered twenty-seven, and he was slipping fast. Nancy and Chuck Sr. signed the papers authorizing the hospital to distribute their son's organs once he died.

If he was not to survive, the McGiverns wanted to be with their son in his last hours. They took up residence in Children's Hospital, located on Thirty-fourth Street. Chuck was in an isolation chamber just down the hall from the family waiting room where Nancy and Chuck Sr. spent most of their time. Doctors and nurses were with Chuck practically around the clock. Every fifteen minutes one of the McGiverns would go down to check on him.

On Saturday night while Nancy, Chuck Sr., and Nancy's uncle were in the family waiting room with some other worried parents, a young boy about twelve years old walked halfway into the waiting room. He was poorly clothed, sported an old plaid jacket, had shaggy brown hair and wore a pair of black-rimmed glasses. He looked at the McGiverns and then at the TV set and then back at the McGiverns. The little stranger said nothing and walked back out into the hallway. Chuck Sr. thought it odd that a boy his age would be wandering around the hospital at that hour, but he let it pass. He had more important things to think about.

Around that same time Nancy went down to check on her son, as the family members were doing regularly. She found that the medal of St. John Neumann had been turned face down. She unhooked the safety pin and turned it face up again. She left the room. When she returned fifteen minutes later she discovered the St. John Neumann medal face down again. She changed it back, right side up. This happened a third time.

She thought that the stress was getting to her. Nancy asked her husband to accompany her to Chuck's room. Together they found the St. John Neumann medal face down. In order to do this one had to unhook the pin, take one medal off, flip the St. John Neumann medal over, rethread the medals and attach the pin to the pillow again. The McGiverns quizzed the nurses, doctors and family members. All denied tampering with the pin.

On Sunday night Nancy was sitting in her son's room. Her chair was away from the door. Unintentionally she overheard the nurses speaking of Chuck in the hall, "It's a shame, he's not going to make it." They didn't know Mrs.

McGivern was in the room. Fighting back a burst of tears, Nancy turned away from the door so as to remain hidden. When she turned her head, she was surprised to see an eight-inch by ten-inch picture of St. John Neumann haphazardly attached to the wall with masking tape. Once again she made inquiries. No one could explain how it got there.

On Monday night the doctors informed the McGiverns that Chuck now also had pneumonia.

On Tuesday morning there was no change in his condition. Later that day a nurse came to the waiting room asking for the McGiverns. "Mr. McGivern," she said, "We had a little problem today which we think you should know about. Two doctors were working in your son's room and one of them looked up and saw a little boy in the doorway. The doctor asked him what he was doing there and the boy replied, 'I came to visit Chuck.' Do you have any idea who this boy might be?" The McGiverns were puzzled.

What perplexed the doctors was how this boy could have penetrated hospital security all the way to Chuck's isolation ward. The doctors called security. They reported a boy at large fitting the following description: about twelve years old, shaggy brown hair, wearing an old plaid jacket and black-rimmed glasses. It was the same boy Chuck Sr. had seen in the waiting room on Saturday night.

Security searched the hospital. The boy could not be found. Chuck Sr. whispered to his wife, "Something strange is going on."

Shortly after that Fr. Robert Roncase of St. Martin of Tours church, the McGiverns' parish priest, arrived. He administered the Sacrament of the Sick to Chuck. Nancy happened to be in the shower at the time. Everyone felt the end was near.

As Nancy was drying her hair a nurse called for her: "Mrs. McGivern, come down and see your son, he just moved!" Nancy and Chuck Sr. rushed down to the room, and by now their son was moving his arm. By 8:00 PM that night his color had returned and he was nodding yes and no to their questions.

At 11:30 PM Chuck Sr. couldn't hold back any longer. He asked his son, "Was there a little boy in here to see you?" Yes, Chuck answered. He had a vivid dream that he was in a hospital bed surrounded by his family, many Asian children who brought him gifts, and an older boy of about twelve who wore black-rimmed glasses. In his dream this boy was Chuck's best friend.

Chuck continued to improve. He was home by Saturday, a week to the day that he was admitted to Children's Hospital.

Today Chuck is seventeen years old, a straight-A student and a fine athlete. He is quiet by nature and not inclined to talk much about these events. Chuck has a deep personal devotion to St. John Neumann, and to his

Church. But when asked if he will become a priest he responds, "I don't think so, but I can't rule anything out in the future."

Nancy and Chuck Sr. are private people too. They often wonder why this favor was bestowed upon them. Nancy says, "My kid is nobody special. I get mad at him like any other mom." Even though the McGiverns tend to be reserved, they feel an obligation to tell the story when asked, because others are helped by it so much. As Nancy puts it, "He is the forgotten saint, and yet he is so close to us."

There is a postscript to this story. When the McGiverns went to the St. John Neumann shrine to give thanks for their son's recovery, they of course brought Chuck along. After they finished their prayers the McGiverns were offered a tour of the little museum. It holds various artifacts and personal possessions of St. John Neumann held and revered by the Redemptorist priests and brothers. Hanging on one of the museum walls is a picture of a child with shaggy brown hair. When Chuck caught sight of it his face broke into a smile. "That was my best friend in my dream, Mom!" he yelled as he pointed to the picture. The priest who was giving them the tour was surprised. "That's interesting, Chuck. That picture was John Neumann when he was twelve," explained the priest. ∎

Chuck McGivern of Northeast Philadelphia was cured of the fatal
children's disease called Reye's Syndrome in 1983. The photo above was
taken of Chuck in 1982.

APPENDIX
I

MIRACLES

In theological terms a miracle is an extraordinary event, produced by God in a religious context which is beyond the powers of corporeal nature, or at least extremely unlikely from the standpoint of those powers alone. Such events are a sign of supernatural activity.

Pope Benedict XIV set the conditions for the official acceptance of a miracle in his classic work on the Beatification and Canonization Process in the mid 1700's, and essentially these conditions still stand today. They are:

1) The illness must be serious and difficult to cure.
2) The illness must not be in its final phase.
3) No remedy must have been taken during the illness, or if it has it must be shown to be ineffective.
4) The cure must be instantaneous.
5) The cure must be complete.
6) There must have been no crisis which may have acted as a catalyst for the cure.
7) The cure must be permanent.[1]

This demonstrates the traditional caution the Church employs in officially recognizing miracles. For example, these requirements have been in use at Lourdes, France for decades. The review process for a single alleged miracle is eight to twelve years. Despite this rigor, cures have been pronounced miraculous by the Church. They are a small percentage of the total number presented for examination.

---

[1] Klappenburg, Bonaventure, O.F.M., *Pastoral Practice and the Paranormal*, trans. David Smith (Franciscan Herald Press, Chicago, Ill., 1979), p. 134-135.

Of the hundreds of miracles claimed to have been obtained through the intercession of St. John Neumann, only three have been evaluated and accepted in accord with the rigorous Canonization standards. The following are the miracles which satisfied those required for his Canonization. They were quite celebrated in the media at the time of their occurrence. They are:

I. ITALIAN GIRL, ELEVEN, IS CURED OF ACUTE PERITONITIS

In May, 1923, eleven-year-old Eva Benassi of Sassuolo, Italy was stricken with acute diffused peritonitis. By the time her family's physician, Dr. Louis Barbanti, correctly diagnosed Eva's condition, she was beyond medical help.

On a Monday morning a priest gave Eva the last rites. That afternoon Dr. Barbanti told Mr. Benassi that Eva would not live through the night.

Sister Elizabeth Romoli, a teacher at the school Eva attended, decided to pray to Bishop Neumann for Eva's recovery. Sister Elizabeth credited Bishop Neumann with her father's recovery from an illness and felt that Neumann might also help Eva.

While praying to Neumann, Sister touched Eva's swollen abdomen with a picture of the Philadelphia Bishop. Her community of nuns and the Benassi family also prayed to Bishop Neumann.

That night the peritonitis disappeared.

In December 1960, in the final examination of her case, before the beatification of Bishop Neumann, Eva, forty-eight, and the mother of two children, was in perfect health.

The Vatican Medical College stated that Eva's cure was instantaneous, perfect, lasting, and "naturally unexplainable."

II. NINETEEN-YEAR-OLD VILLANOVAN SAVED AFTER CAR ACCIDENT

On the evening of July 8, 1949, nineteen-year-old Kent Lenahan of Villanova, Pennsylvania was standing on the running board of a moving car. Suddenly the car swerved out of control, crushing Lenahan against a utility pole.

When he arrived at Bryn Mawr Hospital his skull was crushed, his collarbone was broken, one of his lungs was punctured by a rib, he was bleeding from ears, nose and mouth, and he was comatose. His temperature was 107°, his pulse 160.

A few hours after being admitted to the hospital, doctors treating Lenahan decided there was no hope for his recovery, and ceased medical treatment. His parents refused to believe that no one could help their son.

They went to the Bishop Neumann Shrine and prayed for his recovery. A neighbor gave them a piece of Neumann's cassock. Shortly after the Lenahans touched their son with the cloth, J. Kent Lenahan began to recover from his injuries. His temperature dropped to 100°, his pulse dropped to normal. Less than five weeks after the accident Lenahan walked unaided from the hospital.

Now a music teacher in Pennsylvania, J. Kent Lenahan has only one explanation for being alive today: "They couldn't explain what happened, so I guess it was the Man upstairs."

III. BOY'S CANCER DISAPPEARS
AFTER PRAYERS TO
BISHOP NEUMANN

After months of treatment for osteomyelits, a bone inflammation, doctors found in July 1963 that six-year-old Michael Flanigan of West Philadelphia had Ewing's Sarcoma, a usually lethal form of bone cancer.

Doctors gave Michael six months to live.

The cancer, virtually incurable when it spreads beyond the initial diseased area, had spread from the youth's right tibia to his jaw and lungs.

"If a similar case came to me today," a doctor who recently studied Michael's case commented, "I'd have to say that any chance of survival would be less than zero."

When doctors notified Michael's parents that their son had virtually no chance of recovering from the disease, Mr. and Mrs. John Flanigan decided to take Michael to the Bishop Neumann Shrine at St. Peter's Church, Fifth Street and Girard Ave.

After several visits to the Shrine, Michael began to make a dramatic recovery. No signs of cancer were found in his jaw and lungs by October 1963. By Christmas, 1963, when Michael was supposed to be dead or close to death, all signs of Ewing's Sarcoma had vanished.

In December 1975, after a final examination of Michael's medical records the Medical Board of the Vatican Congregation for the Causes of Saints declared that Michael Flanigan's cure was "scientifically and medically unexplainable," and attributed it to the intercession of Bishop Neumann.

It was this miracle which paved the way towards sainthood for the Philadelphia Bishop.

★   ★   ★   ★

But many of the cases reviewed in this book would have difficulty passing the scrutiny of Pope Benedict's criteria. First, each one would require a tremendous effort specified by church law involving a formal commission of priests, canon lawyers, theologians, physician, surgeons and extensive testimony and examination of the witnesses, a thorough analysis of the medical records, etc. Such an effort takes years, must follow exact procedures, and is usually initiated in conjunction with some specific eclesiastical purpose like canonization. After canonization, miracles no longer warrant official confirmation.

Second, Pope Benedict's insistence that no remedy be applied during the illness, or that it has to be shown ineffective, is hard to comply with today. Virtually no illness goes untreated. As soon as a person falls ill in our country, he is usually put under a doctor's care and medicine is prescribed. If the illness is serious, all manner of medical attention is immediately given to the sick person. This is one of the great benefits of our wealthy and advanced society. Assigning responsibility for a cure then becomes very complex.

Third, the requirement that the cure be instantaneous, taken in its strictest sense (i.e., a matter of seconds or minutes), would cause most cures to fail the test.

But there is a wider view accepted by many Catholic theologians in which a miracle need not be strictly beyond the powers of corporeal nature but only extremely unlikely from the standpoint of those powers alone. The emphasis here would be on the religious context in which the cures take place. In this broader view, even if immediate supernatural intervention is not obvious, but the cures resulted from an extraordinary combination of factors providentially arranged by God, one might be able to legitimately describe them as miraculous. In these instances the healings bespeak God's compassion, which is the symbolic value of any miracle.[2]

---

[2] "Miracles," New Catholic Encyclopedia, Catholic University of America, Washington, DC, (Jack Heraty and Asso., Inc.), Palatine, Ill., 1981, Vol. 9, p. 891-892.

According to this definition many of the cases narrated in this text would meet the grade. Several convergent factors contribute to making these favors fit the parameters of the wider prescription of a miracle:

1) Many physicians have verified the extraordinary, even miraculous recoveries of the subjects involved.

2) The medical records are extant and accessible to all interested parties.

3) Many primary and secondary witness corroborate the claims.

4) The recipients have been willing to put their testimonies in writing and to open up their private lives to investigation.

5) Hospitals, physicians, dates, full names, and places of residence of the recipients have all been identified to make verification possible.

6) In many cases the treatments were ineffective, simply a token effort by frustrated doctors.

Although complete healings are ideal, it is also true that partial (i.e., near complete) healings have given the recipients life, and the opportunity to pursue the love of God, family, friends and others, as well as happiness on many other levels. The excellent quality of their lives, despite their disabilities, is beyond question.

It is important to note that devotion to St. John Neumann and specific prayers to him, as well as the use of his relics, factor heavily in all of these stories. As to the immediacy of the cures, even two of the cures accepted as miracles for St. John Neumann's canonization extend over a period of weeks. It is the favors themselves and the religious context in which they were generated that speaks most profoundly to those who received them. Their lives and the lives of their family and friends, and in some cases even their physicians, were changed forever. A great increase in the virtues of faith and zeal now characterize their lives. Certainly no one could tell Marie Milano or Donna Spadaccini that St. John Neumann didn't win a smile from heaven for them.

In the final analysis it is the extraordinary reverses at the moment of absolute hopelessness, the unexplainable recoveries in the face of imminent death or disaster that garner mounting evidence in favor of God's intervention and personal care for his people. Miracles will always be questioned, but faith stirred anew in the hearts of thousands as a result of the intercession of St. John Neumann is an undeniable fact. ■

APPENDIX

II

HIDDEN FAVORS

While partial cures are very difficult to assess as miraculous, there is another category of divine favors that is virtually impossible to verify — spiritual healings. Spiritual healings, also called inner healings, are cures of the inner person; i.e. healings of the emotions and psyche, memories, conscience and moral faculties, the will, and the soul, etc.

With physical cures, medical data exists to substantiate a claim; in inner healings, however, objective evidence is essentially non-existent. Even if a person feels like "a new creation in Jesus Christ" (2 Cor 5:17), the feeling and testimony are subjective. Behavior changes are equally difficult to quantify or validate.

Many such inner healings have been claimed through the intercession of St. John Neumann. Although a list of these healings could easily be generated, any attempt to verify them would be futile. Nevertheless such testimonies abound, so the faithful are strongly urged to go to St. John Neumann in all their necessities, both spiritual and material. If he can cure cancers of the body, he can surely cure cancers of the soul; as the adage inscribed above the entrance to Our Lady of Lourdes Hospital in Camden, New Jersey reads: "The body is often curable, the soul is ever so." ■

APPENDIX
III

REDEMPTIVE SUFFERING

In the course of Divine Providence, there are many persons who are not healed of their infirmities, despite their most fervent and desperate prayers and petitions. These souls are the chosen of God. For who can truly know Jesus Christ save those who have gone to the cross with him? Christ only asks the most special of souls to be so intimate with him as to be united with him on the cross for the redemption of others. As the Second Vatican Council Fathers put it, "In a special way also, those who are weighed down by poverty, infirmity, sickness and other hardships should realize that they are united to Christ, who suffers for the salvation of the world; let those feel the same who suffer persecution for the sake of justice" (Lumen Gentium #41).

So then, "In bringing about the Redemption through suffering, Christ has raised human suffering to the level of Redemption. Thus each man, in his suffering, can also become a sharer in the redemptive suffering of Christ" (John Paul II, Salvifici Doloris #19).

These are not just sterile theological concepts, but rather the very heart and life of Jesus' message. No one is more endeared or configured to Jesus Christ than the person who cries himself to sleep each night from physical or psychological pain. Whether the suffering soul is by Christ's side at Gethsemani or on the Cross, the spiritual merit of his sufferings united with Christ's have inestimable value.

St. John Neumann knew this truth well. His entire priestly life was one continuum of suffering. This suffering, coupled with his virtue, is why his prayers are so powerful today. May all suffering souls realize their great stature in the eyes of heaven. May they turn to Jesus and the saints for strength and consolation in the midst of their trials. ∎

APPENDIX

IV

VISIONS

In the Catholic Church a supernatural vision is a gift freely and graciously given by God, through which an individual perceives some object that is naturally invisible to man. A true supernatural vision is distinguished from illusions or hallucinations caused by pathological mental states or diabolical influence. Saints Augustine, Thomas Aquinas, John of the Cross and Teresa of Avila divided visions into three categories: corporeal, imaginative and intellectual.

In a corporeal vision, also called an apparition, the eyes perceive an object that is normally invisible to the sense of sight. According to Catholic Tradition, a supernatural corporeal vision could be caused directly by God or mediately through an angelic power.

An imaginative vision is a phantasm supernaturally caused in the imagination without the aid of sight. It may occur during sleep, or in waking hours when it is usually accompanied by ecstacy. Theologians use principles of discernment to determine the authenticity of imaginative visions.

An intellectual vision is a simple intuitive knowledge produced supernaturally without the aid of an impressed formal image in the internal or external senses. Only God can produce this special grace in the mind of an individual.[1]

Visions of the saints have been recorded throughout the history of the Church. Such visions are either corporeal or imaginative visions. In accord with the Divine plan then, visions of persons who have left this life are clearly possible.

St. Thomas writes that such a possibility exists within the Divine economy:

[1] "Visions," New Catholic Encyclopedia, Catholic University of America, Washington, DC, Jack Heraty and Asso., Inc., Palantine Ill., 1981, Vol. 14, p. 717.

According to the disposition of Divine Providence separated souls sometimes come forth from their abode and appear as men ... For even as saints while living in the flesh are able by the gifts of gratuitous grace to heal and work wonders, which can only be done miraculously by the Divine power, and cannot be done by those who lack this gift, so it is not unfitting for the souls of the saints to be endowed with a power in virtue of their glory, so that they are able to appear wondrously to the living.*
(Summa Theological, Suppl. 69.3)

As with all genuine supernatural visions, they are primarily for the good of others. Visions are not proofs of sanctity and are not to be sought or desired by the faithful.

The mere word of a person cannot be taken as certain proof that a vision was supernatural in origin. It is possible for an individual to be mistaken or deceived. Even with devout souls it is possible for the subliminal activity of the subconscious to influence the conscious mind so that a person is unwittingly a victim of illusions.[2]

Caution then is the keynote in visions. But individuals do in fact receive supernatural visions. St. Thomas Aquinas himself cites examples of apparitions of saints in his exposition of the spiritual principles underlying such a possibility.

What about the suggestions that St. John Neumann has appeared to certain individuals in recent years? In the case of both Fr. Kelley and Chuck McGivern we have extraordinary physical recoveries and multiple testimonies of visual apprehensions of a person fitting the description of St. John Neumann (i.e., nurses, doctors, roommates, etc.). While the sighting of the saint will always remain in the realm of probability and mystery, the cures will not and neither will the certitude of faith in the hearts and minds of Fr. Kelley and the McGiverns.   ■

---

* Apparitions of Christ and Mary are represented under a different spiritual principle than the saints, in St. Thomas Aquinas' view.

[2] "Visions," New Catholic Encyclopedia, ibid.

APPENDIX
V

A BRIEF BIOGRAPHY OF ST. JOHN NEUMANN

The ancient village of Prachatitz is located in Bohemia, now southwestern Czechoslovakia, near the borders of Germany and Austria. On March 28, 1811, John Nepomucene Neumann was born the third child and first son of Philip and Agnes Neumann. His father, a Bavarian, owned a small stocking mill and was a village official. His mother was a devout Czech.

Young John showed great promise in his studies and zeal for learning. As he grew older he was undecided about his career, although he was leaning toward medicine. In 1831, at the advice of his mother, he applied to the school of theology at Budweis. John was surprised at being accepted since the application process was so competitive. From that moment on, he never gave another thought to medicine.

While excelling in theology at Budweis, John also studied languages on the side. Besides his native German and Bohemian, he became accomplished in Italian, Spanish, Greek, Latin, English and French. Later in life he even taught himself Gaelic in order to minister to Irish immigrants.

During his years in theology school, urgent appeals came from the United States for missionaries to tend to the spiritual needs of Germans who had emigrated to the big Eastern cities there. John conceived a strong and lively desire to serve there as a priest. The idea almost became an obsession with him.

When he finished his theological studies there was a glut of priests in his diocese, and his ordination was indefinitely deferred. He resolved to abandon all to Divine Providence. Taking leave of his family he crossed western Europe and took passage on an overcrowded ship destined for Ellis Island, New York.

At twenty-five years old he found himself in the center of Manhattan alone, not ordained and without a single friend.

The next day he was warmly welcomed to the Diocese of New York by Bishop John DuBois. Bishop DuBois reviewed Neumann's transcripts and was delighted to have him. The bishop was in dire need of German-speaking priests. He ordained him three weeks later in New York City on June 25, 1836.

Fr. Neumann then began a series of assignments to serve the German Catholic communities in the backwoods settlements of upstate New York. These included Buffalo, Niagara Falls, Williamsville, Erie, Batamia, and North Bush. But four years of this migratory life in these rugged forests and farmlands proved too lonely for Fr. Neumann. He longed for priestly companionship.

Neumann observed the Redemptorist priests who also worked in upstate New York and was attracted by their fraternal spirit and apostolic zeal. He felt that he needed the mutual priestly support of a religious congregation in order to persevere effectively as a missionary. Fr. Neumann's complete physical collapse, which left him unable to attend to his duties for three months in the summer of 1840, may also have been a factor in his decision to join the Redemptorists.

In November 1840 Fr. John Neumann took the habit of the Redemptorist Congregation. He was the first cleric to pronounce his vows as a Redemptorist in the United States. As a Redemptorist priest he served in Maryland and Pittsburgh until his health was broken once again. He was sent to Baltimore to recover.

While convalescing in Baltimore, Neumann was shocked to hear that he was ordered to serve as the temporary superior of all Redemptorists in the United States. He was thirty-five years old and only five years a Redemptorist. The order had come from the Redemptorist headquarters in Europe. Neumann filled this position for two years and was then made pastor of a large church in downtown Baltimore.

In 1851 the new Archbishop of Baltimore, James Patrick Kenrick, arrived. He had just finished twenty years as bishop of Philadelphia. It did not take long for Archbishop Kenrick to become aware of Fr. Neumann's outstanding qualities. Kenrick recommended him for the next bishop of Philadelphia. Fr. Neumann was badly shaken by the prospect and did all he could to resist the possibility by appealing to Kenrick and his Redemptorist superiors in Rome.

Over his objections, John Nepomucene Neumann was consecrated Bishop of Philadelphia in March 28, 1852. Neumann obediently undertook the direction of the vast, populated and burgeoning diocese of Philadelphia. During the next and final eight years of his life, despite his weak physical composition and fierce resistance from certain quarters, Bishop Neumann attempted to the best of his ability to serve the diocese of Philadelphia. At the time he took office, his diocese also included Allentown, Johnstown, Harrisburg, Scranton, Camden, Trenton and Wilmington.

Some said that Neumann, short of stature and somewhat lacking in sophistication, was a poor administrator and had not the proper dignity and demeanor to be a prelate of a cosmopolitan metropolis like Philadelphia. His simple and modest deportment was scorned and disdained by some of the monied class of Philadelphia.

But at the end of his eight years, when his accomplishments for God and the Church of Philadelphia were tallied, they were formidable. Bishop Neumann administered the largest diocese in the country; he held three diocesan synods, enacted legislation for priests and people; made investigations of liturgical practices; instilled a vigorous piety into the faithful by means of the Forty Hours Devotions, missions, creations of confraternities and religious societies; engaged in legal battles for church property; organized a diocesan school system and saw at least thirty-five new schools arise; built eighty churches in the diocese of Philadelphia; conducted visitation tours in pioneer settlements; wrote a catechism and a Bible history; was in the forefront of Catholic educational efforts and the parochial school system in the United States; took an active part in one plenary and two provincial councils; and was present in Rome and participated in the ceremonies for the formal promulgation for the dogma of the Immaculate Conception: all this before he was fifty years of age. At the same time he continued to apply himself assiduously to his own spiritual life.

The holy Bishop died on January 5, 1860. All of Philadelphia wept. He was canonized a saint in Rome by Pope Paul VI on June 19, 1977. All of Philadelphia rejoiced. ■

BIOGRAPHICAL REFERENCES

1) Berger, Fr. John A., C.SS.R., *Life of Right Rev. John N. Neumann*. Benziger Bros., New York, 1884.
2) Curley, Fr. Michael J., C.SS.R. *Bishop John Neumann, C.SS.R.* Bishop Neumann Center, Philadelphia, 1952.
3) Galvin, James, C.SS.R., *St. John Neumann*, Helican Press, Baltimore, 1964.
4) Hindman, Jane F., *An Ordinary Saint*, Arena Lettres, New York, 1977.
5) Rush, Alfred C., C.SS.R., trans., *The Autobiography of St. John Neumann*, Daughters of St. Paul, Boston, 1977.
6) Turbet, Paschal, C.SS.R., *The Little Bishop*, Daughters of St. Paul, Boston, 1977.
7) Wilson, Robert H., *St. John Neumann*, Institutional Services, Inc., Philadelphia, 1977.

ADDITIONAL BIBLIOGRAPHY

1) Douglas, Philip, *Saint of Philadelphia*, Ravengate.
2) Ferrante, Nicola, C.SS.R., *S. Giovanni Neumann* (Italian), Pisani, Rome.
3) Flavius, Brother, C.S.C., *House on Logan Square*, Dujarie Press.
4) Kolacek, Josef, S.J., *Der Heilige der Neuen Welt* (German), Christiana Verlag, Germany.
5) Langan, Tom, *Harvester of Souls*, Sunday Visitor.
6) Litkowski, Sr. Pelagia, O.P., *Friend To All*, Growth Unlimited.
7) Murphy, Rev. Francis X., C.SS.R., *John N. Neumann Saint*, Erra Press.
8) Sheehan, Elizabeth Odell, *John Neumann, Children's Bishop*, Vision Books.

NINE-DAY PRAYER
Imploring
Saint John Neumann's
Intercession

1st Day –

O Saint John Neumann, obtain for me a lively faith in all the truths that the Holy Roman Catholic Church teaches, together with the divine light to know the vanity of all earthly things, and the hideousness of my sins. Obtain for me also the special favor which I now ask through your intercession with God.

Let us pray

O Lord, Who on earth both praised and practiced the hidden life, grant that, in these days of pride and outward display, the humble ways of Your Servant, Saint John Neumann, may inspire us to imitate Your divine example.

Teach us, O Divine Master, to be like Your servant, the holy bishop; intent on pleasing only You and on performing our good actions free from the desire to be seen and glorified by men.

That his holy example may influence an ever increasing number of souls, grant, O Lord, the favors we ask through his intercession. Amen.

2nd Day—

O Saint John Neumann, obtain for me the firm hope of receiving from God, through the merits of Jesus Christ and the intercession of Mary and your prayers the pardon of my sins, final perseverance and paradise. Obtain for me also the special favor which I now ask through your intercession with God.

Let us pray: O Lord, etc.

3rd Day—

O Saint John Neumann, obtain for me an ardent love of God, that will detach me from the love of created things and from myself, to love Him alone and to spend myself for His glory. Obtain for me also the special favor which I now ask through your intercession with God.

Let us pray: O Lord, etc.

4th Day—

O Saint John Neumann, obtain for me perfect resignation to the will of God, that I may accept in peace, sufferings, contempt, persecutions, loss of goods, and reputation, and finally death itself. Obtain for me also the special favor which I now ask through your intercession with God.

Let us pray: O Lord, etc.

5th Day—

O Saint John Neumann, obtain for me a heartfelt sorrow for my sins, that I may never cease to weep over the displeasure I have given my God. Obtain for me also the special favor I now ask through your intercession with God.

Let us pray: O Lord, etc.

6th Day—

O Saint John Neumann, obtain for me a true love of my neighbor, that will make me do good even to those who have offended me. Obtain for me also the special favor which I now ask through your intercession with God.

Let us pray: O Lord, etc.

7th Day —

O Saint John Neumann, obtain for me the virtue of holy purity and the help required to resist impure temptations by invoking the holy names of Jesus and Mary. Obtain for me also the special favor which I now ask through your intercession with God.

Let us pray: O Lord, etc.

8th Day —

O Saint John Neumann, obtain for me a tender devotion to the Passion of Jesus Christ, to the Blessed Sacrament, and to my dear Mother Mary. Obtain for me also the special favor which I now ask through your intercession with God.

Let us pray: O Lord, etc.

9th Day —

O Saint John Neumann, obtain for me above all the grace of final perseverance and the grace always to pray for it, especially in time of temptation and at the hour of death. Obtain for me also the special favor which I now ask through your intercession with God.

Let us pray: O Lord, etc.

Imprimatur:

JOHN J. KROL, ARCHBISHOP OF PHILADELPHIA

PRAYER

O my God, I adore Your infinite Majesty with all the powers of my soul. I thank You for the graces and gifts which You bestowed upon Your faithful servant, Saint John Neumann. I ask You to glorify him also on earth. For this end I beseech You to grant me the favor which I humbly ask from Your Fatherly mercy. Amen.

(3 Our Fathers and 3 Hail Marys)

Nihil Obstat:
Sacred Congregation of Rites

**To Further devotion to Saint John Neumann
join the SAINT JOHN NEUMANN GUILD**

★　　★　　★　　★　　★　　★

For information address:

NATIONAL SHRINE OF SAINT JOHN NEUMANN
1019 N. FIFTH ST., PHILADELPHIA, PA. 19123
(215)-627-3080

PLAN A PILGRIMAGE

THE NATIONAL SHRINE OF ST. JOHN NEUMANN is located at St. Peter's Church, 1019 N. Fifth Street, Philadelphia, Pennsylvania 19123. The Shrine has been a place of pilgrimage for more than a hundred years. Bishop John Neumann, Fourth Bishop of Philadelphia, had often expressed the wish that after his death he be buried with his Redemptorist brethren in the crypt below the church. In the course of the years the bodies of deceased Redemptorists were transferred to Holy Redeemer Cemetery in Philadelphia, but the body of Bishop Neumann remained under the sanctuary of the Shrine Church.

At the time of the Beatification, his remains were exhumed, authenticated and redressed in the Bishop's vestments and placed in a glass case under the main altar, where they remain today for all to see. Pilgrims still come from all over to beg the Saint's intercession.

Novena services are held daily. There is a museum and gift shop for the convenience of visitors. Membership in the ST. JOHN NEUMANN GUILD entitles one to remembrance in more than seventy Masses a year plus a copy of the St. John Neumann *NEWSLETTER* containing items of interest to St. John Neumann clients. See next page for information and a schedule of devotions.

THE NATIONAL SHRINE OF ST. JOHN NEUMANN

1019 North Fifth Street Philadelphia, PA 19123

Open Daily 7:30 AM to 6:00 PM
Sunday 7:30 AM to 5:00 PM

GROUP VISIT PROGRAM

Welcome - Prayers - Veneration of Relic - Blessing of Sick

Visit to Museum and Gift Shop

Call (215) 627-3080

Weekday Masses at Shrine: 7:30 AM, 12:15 and 5:30 PM

Novena Devotions in Honor of St. John Neumann:
Every day (except Sunday) 12:15 PM (with Mass)
Sunday 3:00 PM (with Mass)

St. John Neumann Museum Open:
Daily 9:00 AM to 5:00 PM

St. John Neumann Gift Shop:
Monday through Saturday 9:00 AM to 4:00 PM
Sunday 10:00 AM to 4:00 PM

Family Radio Rosary - WIBF - FM (104):
Weekdays at 1:30 PM
Saturdays at 9:00 PM
Sundays at 7:30 PM
Dial (215)-627-6110 for Today's Spiritual Message

*   *   *   *   *   *

Prayer to invoke God's favor through the intercession of
St. John Neumann

O my God, I adore Your infinite majesty with all the powers of my soul. *
I thank You for the graces and gifts which You have bestowed upon Your
faithful Servant, Saint John Neumann. * I ask You to glorify him also on
earth. * For this end I beseech You to grant me the favor which I humbly ask
from Your fatherly mercy. Amen.

In the event that you do receive some special extraordinary favor through
the intercession of St. John Neumann it would be gratefully appreciated if
you would kindly notify:

St. John Neumann Shrine
1019 N. 5th Street
Philadelphia, PA 19123
(215) 627-3080